The Minister's Handbook for Personal Finance

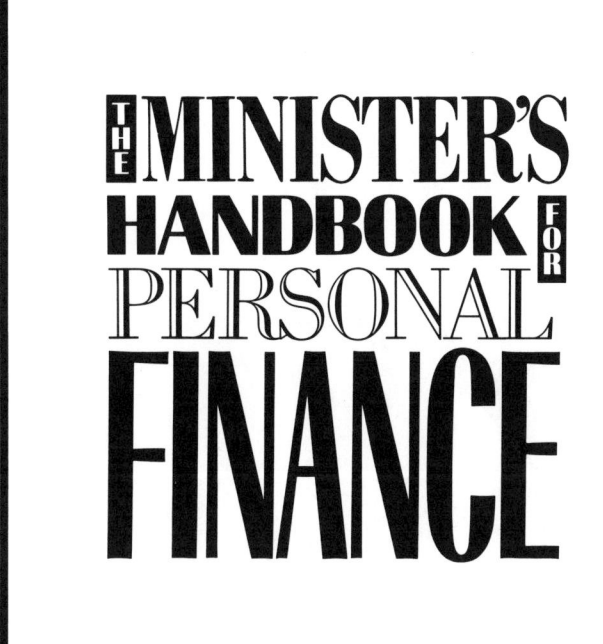

MANFRED HOLCK JR.

AUGSBURG   **MINNEAPOLIS**

THE MINISTER'S HANDBOOK FOR PERSONAL FINANCE

Copyright © 1990 Augsburg Fortress. All rights reserved. Except for brief quotations in critical articles or reviews, no part of this book may be reproduced in any manner without prior written permission from the publisher. Write to: Permissions, Augsburg Fortress, 426 S. Fifth St., Box 1209, Minneapolis, MN 55440.

Permission is granted for readers to reproduce pages 18, 57, 58, and Worksheets 1–8, provided copies are for local or personal use and the credit line on the page also appears on all copies.

Cover and internal design: Rudd

Library of Congress Cataloging-in-Publication Data
Holck, Manfred.
    The minister's handbook for personal finance / by Manfred Holck,
Jr.
      p.   cm.
    Includes bibliographical references.
    ISBN 0-8066-2459-0 (alk. paper)
    1. Clergy—Finance, Personal—Handbooks, manuals, etc.   I. Title.
BV4397.H585   1990
332.024'2—dc20   90-32827
                                                                                                                                                     CIP

The paper used in this publication meets the minimum requirements of American National Standard for Information Sciences—Permanence of Paper for Printed Library Materials, ANSI Z329.48-1984.

Manufactured in the U.S.A.   AF 9-2459

94   93   92   91   90   1   2   3   4   5   6   7   8   9   10

Contents

Introduction   7

1. The Compensation Package—Guidelines and Tax Considerations   9

2. Budgeting for Family Spending   23

3. Credit Control   33

4. Sensible Investing   37

5. Insurance for Ministers   44

6. Housing for Ministers   52

7. Social Security for Ministers   61

8. Planning Retirement Income   70

Bibliography   78

Worksheets   79

Introduction

It's no secret. Many ministers and their families struggle to make ends meet from month to month. Those with generous pay packages don't worry so much; those with less-than-adequate compensation worry a lot. And for some, the problem of balancing the checkbook is a struggle that just won't end.

This book is written for ministers and their families who are struggling to stretch scarce dollars. It is also intended to provide suggestions on how to save a little money. Since you picked up this book, you may indeed be one of those for whom these pages are intended. The eight chapters and the worksheets that go with them are intended to help you with that goal. I don't promise miracles, but I will share with you ideas that have worked for other people and that have always been helpful to my family.

Chapter 1 contains the kind of information that you may want to pass on to those responsible for putting your compensation package together each year. You'll read about how low pay affects your ministry and your relationship with others. There are suggestions for supplemental benefits that could be added to your compensation plan, as well as guidelines for reimbursement of the expenses you incur in the course of your work. I'll also propose some ways to arrange your compensation package so that the share you give to the Internal Revenue Service (IRS) may be less.

Compensation planning.

Many ministerial families yearn to keep up with the Joneses but also have to deal with the constraints of limited resources. It is of the utmost importance to set financial goals and know how to work toward achieving them. In Chapter 2, I'll give you the ten steps involved in making a family budget and describe techniques that can help you meet your current needs and still be able to save for the future.

Financial goals.

You probably have bought things on credit. Most people have. But some people have a bigger debt load than they can handle. Avoiding bad debt-management habits, using credit cards wisely, and getting out of debt is what Chapter 3 is all about.

Credit cards.

Many ministers do not have the cash resources to make investments in the stock market or in financial instruments other than their pension plan. Some suggestions on sensible goals for investment planning on a preacher's pay are given in Chapter 4.

Investing.

It's often surprising how little insurance some ministers carry. You may not know much about insurance, but you should protect yourself and your family from financial disaster by making certain that your

Insurance.

insurance package—health, life, liability, and property—is what it ought to be. Chapter 5 tells you what you will want to consider.

Housing allowance.

The Internal Revenue Service allows the rental value of the parsonage or the amount of the minister's housing allowance to be excluded from taxable income to the extent that it is used to provide a home. It's important that you understand the tax laws with regard to housing and take full advantage of them. Chapter 6 explains how to maximize your housing allowance.

Social security.

Ministers pay the self-employment social security tax, which is 15.3 percent beginning in 1990. That's simply a lot of money, and it's on your total salary *plus* the value of housing. Of course, social security benefits can be generous, including retirement, lifetime health coverage, disability if you need it, and even survivors' benefits, too. Chapter 7 explains the advantages and costs of the program, discusses benefit calculations, and considers the conscientious objection to social security chosen by some clergy.

Retirement income.

Wise ministers start planning for retirement income as soon as they are ordained. At age 55 it's almost too late; age 25 is better. Chapter 8 wraps up this book with some helpful ideas on how to plan your retirement income, no matter your age.

I hope you'll find the information in this book interesting and, above all, helpful. If your frustration about making ends meet is not tempered by some of these suggestions, write to me about your situation. Maybe there's some further way I can assist you. My address is 2450 Stratford Dr., Austin, TX 78746. It'll only cost you a stamp.

Manfred Holck Jr.

1

Your Compensation Package—Guidelines and Tax Considerations

Depending on the decade and the denomination, competition may be great or nonexistent for parish ministers. Supply and demand will greatly affect the compensation you can expect. It could also determine whether or not you have a job in ministry. Tight supply gives you an opportunity to ask for more pay more easily. A surplus supply of eligible ministers makes the task of finding adequate pay much more difficult. Although you may be convinced that pay should be related to your ability to perform effectively as a minister, it doesn't always happen that way.

Supply and demand may affect pay.

Your compensation package affects you, your family, and your job performance in many ways. Adequate compensation makes life easier, of course. So, before discussing the elements of an adequate compensation package, let's look at the effects of low pay on the ministry.

THE EFFECTS OF LOW PAY

I've been in the ministry long enough (maybe you have, too) to remember back when pay was really low—$300 a month in cash, an adequate house, and all the fresh vegetables, meat, and eggs that I could garner on a round of calling. Not much money, even then, but we ate well and the doctors were free.

What level of pay is sufficient? For some, $50,000 may be low pay because they have found ways to spend it all. For others, $25,000 may be good pay because they know how to manage their resources. But low pay is difficult anytime. Here's what it does to you, your family, and your ministry.

What is low pay?

Low Pay Affects Your Job Performance

Ministry is hard enough without the added burden of worrying about how to pay the bills. Going with low pay too long will interfere with

Low pay, bills, and job performance.

effective ministry. It can't be denied that personal money worries exacerbate even the normal pressures of a job. They interfere with efficiency and productivity. The congregation will feel the pinch, too, as ministry goes downhill. If you can't get your mind off your own worries, you will find it hard to provide aid and comfort to others.

Low Pay Affects the Perceptions of Others

In spite of the affluence of some television evangelists, such large incomes are not the norm for the vast majority of ministers. Many people perceive ministers as low-paid employees. That's why clergy can get discounts, reduced doctor's fees, free admissions, and the like. The public's perception (and perhaps expectation) has been that pastors are underpaid.

Such a perception may be a self-fulfilling prophecy. Change the perception, and people change their attitudes. Change people's attitudes about what the pastor's pay should be, and they'll change your pay. When people are convinced that the pastor should not be underpaid but well paid, their attitude toward the minister improves, and their recognition of the importance of the ministry is enhanced. They recognize the pastor as a professional person, trained to minister in a crisis and to offer solace in moments of grief, pain, and sorrow.

Low Pay Affects Your Attitude

In general, I've always had a rather positive attitude toward the church. Maybe that's because I've always been paid an adequate salary—at least one that I thought was fair. I have quickly learned that my grown children can earn far more than I can, and I am pleased that they can. At the same time I know that my pay as a pastor has been fair, equitable, and just. It may not be so for you, however.

Job attitudes and low pay.

Low-paid ministers are likely to develop some negative feelings toward the church that is not treating them fairly. If your pay is low, maybe you already have such feelings. Obviously that's going to affect your attitudes toward ministry, toward your specific job, and toward the people to whom you are supposed to minister.

Most of us would welcome an increase in our pay. I do know some pastors who, as a matter of routine each year, refuse salary increases . . . but they get them anyway! Quite simply, you want to be recognized for the work you do. A generous pay increase would help to improve your attitude immensely.

Inflation Makes Low Pay Worse

There's no question that inflation eats into our pay with regularity. Fortunately, double-digit inflation does not plague us every year; during some years it is next to nothing. Nevertheless, we all know that inflation is a constant, and that ten years from now we'll have to almost double our incomes to maintain our present standard of living.

Therefore, defensive action is necessary to keep from falling further and further behind. If you cannot afford the admission price to take your family to the movies, or the orthodontist's bill is about to blow a hole in what little savings you have, or piano lessons become increasingly difficult to finance, adjustments are called for. Wait for the new movies to become older movies; they'll be cheaper eventually and may even be on TV. Perhaps you can barter with the orthodontist and perform a needed service in partial exchange for a reduction in the bill. Maybe the orthodontist will offer you a discount anyway. Do the same type of bartering with the piano teacher. Sometimes creative arrangements with others can help offset the inevitable rise in the cost of goods and services.

Inflation rate is usually more.

Low Pay Forces Ministers to Moonlight

One survey I recently read stated that more than 24 percent of Protestant ministers "moonlight" in order to make ends meet. Maybe you have a second job to put more money into the bank. But because such activity takes time from ministry, you must ask whether the congregation suffers and your ministry is less effective. Must you (and should you) hold down a second job?

Some people never have enough money no matter how much they earn, and they always want more. They work at extra jobs because it generates more spendable income. Yet one full-time job consumes enough time away from the family. Another job only makes that time away even worse. Besides, ministry is not a forty-hour-a-week job anyway; it's more like sixty hours a week. Time for a second job is severely limited. Yet, some pastors make room in their schedules for it because they say they have to. Moonlighting is an unhappy solution to the vexing problem of low pay. With careful money management, perhaps it is something that you can avoid.

Part-time work.

Low Pay Forces Spouses to Work

More than half of the spouses of ministers are employed for pay outside the home, and the percentage continues to increase. In one survey, respondents indicated that the spouse is employed simply to boost family income. For most it's a case of necessity.

Spousal income.

With more and more two-paycheck families in our country, this news is not surprising. It's a situation common not only to the ministry but to other occupations as well. Many spouses, of course, work at fulfilling careers of their choice. Nevertheless, when both spouses work, there is added stress and more time spent away from the family. Child care often becomes an important consideration. If low pay forces a spouse to work, there may be dissatisfaction.

Low Pay Can Affect Pensions

In a recent issue of *The Clergy Journal*,[1] noted writer and preacher Lyle E. Schaller pointed out that policy decisions being made now

---

[1] Lyle E. Schaller, "Policy Questions about Your Pension Program," *The Clergy Journal LXV, 6 (1989):* 44.

by denominational pension boards will affect the financial future of both ministers and congregations for decades to come. Among those policy decisions are ones that affect ministers' retirement incomes. Depending on the retirement policies adopted, funding costs could cut sharply into congregational budgets, have an impact on current compensation paid, and, down the road, affect ministerial pensions dramatically.

Every pastor needs to be concerned about income during retirement, that time in life when salary is no longer coming in. Early planning is essential to developing a comfortable plan. And low pay has an effect in this area, too. As is so often true, those ministers with the larger salaries will be the ones with the larger retirement incomes.

Low pay, low retirement income.

Rather than waiting to find out what your pension is going to be, now is the time to learn what you can expect and to make appropriate alternative plans. Chapter 8 will give you more information about what you can do. For the moment, consider that if your current salary is low, your retirement pension will probably also be low. To boost that pension, you'll have to take some dramatic financial action soon.

Low Pay Forces Some Out of the Ministry

My guess is that if your low pay continues for too long, you'll be looking around for something else, and it won't be parish ministry. If you can't afford to live on the pay your congregation offers and something else turns up, you will wish to make a change. But it's a sad situation for the church to lose any one of its well-trained ministers because pay was too low. Perhaps the ideas in this book will help you manage your resources and give you information about an adequate compensation package that you can take to your congregation.

The Remedy for Low Pay

Let me hasten to say that not all pastors are in dire financial straits, as this discussion might suggest. Most of us are able to muddle through. But if you can't stretch your paycheck month after month, you must either cut your spending or raise your income. You don't need a book to tell you that. What you may need, however, is some advice about how that can be done without leaving ministry or just giving up. The following pages offer suggestions on how you can spend your resources more wisely, conserve your resources more effectively, and generally do a better job of managing your money.

YOUR COMPENSATION PLAN

The arrangement of your compensation plan determines your income and affects the amount of income tax you pay, often quite dramatically. Here are ideas that seem to provide the greatest take-home pay, offer the best tax advantages, and satisfy congregational lay leaders.

Reimbursements

One of the fundamental principles followed in any good compensation plan for a church worker is full reimbursement of all professional expenses. It is a basic right of an employee to be paid in full for any out-of-pocket expenses incurred on behalf of the employer. Unless you're receiving full reimbursement, your own salary is probably being cut short by expenses on behalf of your employer. It also means that you're paying proportionally more income tax. Once your congregation has adopted a principle of full reimbursement, the rest of the plan should follow smoothly.

Full reimbursement of all professional expenses.

Professional Costs.
Your goal is full reimbursement of those costs that you incur as pastor of your congregation in order to get your job done. These are costs for the benefit of your congregation, as well as for you. They include transportation, church supplies, gifts to members, books, subscriptions to professional journals, continuing education, dues, and so on.

Once again, please keep in mind that reimbursements are precisely that—reimbursements, not compensation. These are congregational costs for ministry. They show up on your church's budget as an expense item (perhaps a large expense) but they are not compensation. Be sure that the distinction is kept clearly in mind.

Car Expenses.
The largest of all of your professional expenses is probably the cost of using a personal automobile on church business. Your congregation will have to decide how best to implement the reimbursement plan for this expense.

The ideal arrangement for making certain that your car expenses are covered is for your congregation to provide you with the exclusive use of a church-owned or leased automobile, including the use of a church credit card for gas and oil. That way the church, not the pastor, really assumes all the costs, as it should.

A church-owned car.

The least desirable way for your congregation to pay those expenses is to make an annual payment or a monthly fixed-allowance payment to cover potential expenses. Often that lump-sum payment has no relation to the expenses that you actually incur. It may have been set some years ago and now may be woefully inadequate. You would probably have to dip into salary to pay for some of the costs of operating your own car on church business, which is not equitable.

A better way is for your congregation to pay a cents-per-mile reimbursement. Keep a notebook in your car to record the miles driven. Estimate what it costs you to operate your car per mile, including replacement, and then be sure that you receive that amount as the allowance for miles driven on church business. The arrangement should allow you to tell the treasurer each month how many miles you have driven your car on church business and to receive the reimbursement promptly.

Cents-per-mile reimbursement.

The Internal Revenue Service (IRS) currently does allow 26 cents a mile for the automatic mileage deduction, but that's no assurance that this is the cost of operating a car. It may cost you 25 cents or 30 cents a mile to operate the automobile. If so, that's what you should ask for as reimbursement. If your congregation objects to the rate you tell them, you could suggest that it lease or buy a car for you and pay all costs for it. Then the congregation would know precisely what it costs for you to get around to see the membership. This solution may or may not be within your church's means.

Be aware that the amount of allowance that you receive could make a difference for income tax purposes. Because of the 1986 Tax Reform Act, if you don't receive enough allowance or reimbursement to cover all costs, not all of your excess costs may be deductible for income tax purposes. That's because unreimbursed professional expenses are listed on Schedule A as miscellaneous expenses and are deductible only as they exceed 2 percent of adjusted gross income. It would be better to have a larger allowance than you think you need or specific reimbursement if you want the best tax advantage. (Don't cut your salary to raise the allowance, however; that may reduce pension contributions, thus reducing your future pension. Just have enough allowance added to the reimbursement that you are already receiving to cover costs.)

Government approved automatic allowance.

For tax purposes, the IRS currently permits a 26 cents-per-mile deduction for all business use miles.

Any car allowance you receive is generally considered to be fully taxable income. Expenses may be deducted, however, either at the automatic mileage rate noted previously or at actual cost, including depreciation. Self-employed ministers will list the car-expense deduction on Schedule C. Ministers who are employees and receive an allowance or reimbursement of expenses will show these deductions on Form 2106. Unreimbursed professional expense deductions for the minister as employee will be subject to the limitation of the 2 percent of adjusted gross income rule on Schedule A.

Supplemental Benefits

In addition to the reimbursement of professional expenses, your congregation should provide a variety of supplemental benefits to you, based on your individual needs and those of your family. Most employees receive certain benefits in addition to salary, such as a pension plan, a health plan, insurance, and perhaps other items as well.

Supplemental/fringe benefits are important.

If you are pastor to a rural congregation, the farmers and ranchers on your official board may object to any supplemental benefits because they don't receive them. If you can, help them to understand that you are an employee and that you are not self-employed (even though you do pay the self-employment social security tax). Help them not to confuse their self-employment income with the wages they pay to you. Employees do receive benefits from their employers. Pastors should, too.

There are various supplemental benefits that your congregation may want to consider. Most of them have tax consequences. Not all of the following items are essential, but all can be considered and all are provided to some clergy. Ask your congregation to consider those that will be most helpful to you. Remind your congregation that a supplemental benefit paid by the congregation can often provide a tax benefit that might not be available when paid personally by the pastor.

Pension Plan Contributions. Retirement comes all too quickly for us. Thus, it is important that you be certain your congregation has made adequate plans to pay for and to fund your retirement program.

Most denominations have a pension plan program for their ministers. Many of these are self-funded by a church pension board; others are handled through an insurance company. Potential tax benefits are available to clergy through such plans. Be certain that your congregation's contributions on behalf of your plan are tax deferred so that no tax—income or social security—is currently due on such contributions.

You may want to explore the possibilities of making additional contributions into a tax-deferred annuity (often called a tax-sheltered annuity) by means of a salary reduction plan. Perhaps your congregation might also be willing to go beyond its required contribution. Maximum contributions are generally limited to 20 percent of cash salary. A tax-deferred annuity offers ministers an opportunity to accumulate pension dollars while deferring income tax on the contribution and on the interest the fund earns. The contribution and interest earned on that fund are subject to income tax when received. However, a church pension plan can designate such pension as housing allowance; in such a case, the pension may never be taxable if it is spent to provide a home in retirement.

Additional pension contributions.

In addition to any church pension plan or other deferred annuity, you can participate in an Individual Retirement Account (IRA). Tax-deferred IRA contributions are limited to $2,000 (or earnings, whichever is less) with the possibility of another $2,000 being contributed by the spouse who has earnings. A $2,250 maximum is applicable when the spouse is not employed. Under current tax law, if adjusted gross income on a joint return is more than $50,000, you won't be able to make a tax-deferred contribution unless you are not a participant in an employer-sponsored pension plan. There is no limitation when adjusted gross income is less than $40,000.

IRAs.

Ministers who have self-employment income (rather than salary from a church) may make contributions into a Keogh-type retirement plan. Contributions are generally limited to 20 percent of such income.

Chapter 8 provides more information about planning for retirement.

Health and Disability. No family can afford to be without health insurance, including a major medical plan and disability benefits. The cost of being sick is so high that without insurance, few

Health insurance premiums.

ministers would be able to meet the cost if one of the family were hospitalized even for a short time. Obviously, one never knows when a hospital stay may be necessary; thus, continuous coverage is extremely important to be prepared in the event of an emergency.

Premiums for health coverage should be paid by the congregation. There's an income tax benefit that way, because health insurance premiums paid by an employer are not taxable income. Also, most taxpayers are no longer able to take a medical expense deduction on their tax returns unless they have an extraordinary amount of unreimbursed medical costs. Only those unreimbursed medical expenses exceeding 7.5 percent of adjusted gross income are deductible.

Although social security benefits do include disability coverage, they will probably be inadequate; thus such benefits should be supplemented by your own coverage. That coverage should be the congregation's responsibility, because if family resources are inadequate, a disabled pastor without adequate insurance coverage could become a severe financial burden to a caring congregation.

Group Term Life Insurance. Premiums on a group term life insurance policy for up to $50,000 coverage can be paid for by the congregation without the premiums being taxable income. Any other life insurance premiums paid by the congregation on a policy controlled by the pastor would be taxable income.

Allowance for Social Security Taxes. Of course you pay both income taxes and social security taxes. Yet some lay leaders don't know that. Many congregation members believe that somehow or other, their pastor is exempt from taxes. Not so. In fact, as you are well aware, you pay a good deal more social security tax than anyone else who is an employee in your congregation. And the eventual retirement benefit won't be any more!

Ministers pay self-employment social security tax (SECA).

By law, clergy are required to pay the self-employment social security tax, even though they are employees for income tax purposes. The congregation, as employer, is not required to pay any social security tax on wages paid to the minister, nor can it withhold any social security taxes (as it must do for other employees).

In 1988 and 1989, the rate at which clergy paid the social security tax was 13.02 percent. Other employees paid only 7.56 percent of their income toward that tax. In 1990, clergy pay the social security tax at a rate of 15.3 percent of their income (although one-half of the tax is a business expense deduction, thus reducing the effective rate somewhat), whereas all other employees pay only 7.65 percent.

Thus, the social security tax is a rather significant tax burden for clergy when congregations do not assist in its payment. Because congregations cannot by law pay the tax for the minister, that ever-increasing cost must come out of the pastor's paycheck, reducing net take-home pay even more and doing so at a faster rate than for other employees. Of course, like any other taxpayer, the minister hopes eventually to benefit from the payment of that tax. Retirement benefits, survivor benefits, disability benefits, Medicare, and a death benefit are all possibilities.

Concerned congregations have taken steps to help their pastors meet that cost by providing them with an allowance for the social security tax. That allowance or offset, paid to the pastor, is used to pay the social security tax, or at least part of it. It is taxable income, however, so there is no tax benefit in receiving such an amount. The benefit comes in having the amount stated on the church budget (thus alerting the membership to the fact that the minister pays the tax) and in allowing for an automatic salary increase when the rate goes up.

Social security allowance eases cash flow problems to meet SECA tax.

Medical Expense Reimbursement Plan. A properly developed medical expense reimbursement plan would pay the uninsured medical expenses of the church's employees. Such a benefit would not be taxable income under Section 105 of the Internal Revenue Code provided that a carefully prepared resolution is adopted by the official board for the benefit of all full-time employees. Adapt the sample resolution provided on page 18.

MERP.

Continuing Education. As a minister, you need to keep up with the current trends in theology, counseling, worship, education, evangelism, and stewardship. You want to. Your congregation can provide such an opportunity to you and provide an income tax benefit at the same time by paying for continuing education costs. Both you and your congregation will benefit from such a program. Be sure that your congregation makes at least two weeks' time available (in addition to any vacation). Adequate time and money for helping you to maintain and improve skills in ministry are important for the vitality of your church.

Education costs paid by church.

For income tax purposes, the congregation should pay all continuing education costs. That way, neither the reimbursement nor the expense has to be reported on the tax return. Without reimbursement, any such costs incurred by you would be deductible only on Schedule A and then subject to the 2 percent floor—thus not entirely deductible.

Sabbatical Leave. Many congregations provide a three-month fully paid leave for continuing education after six years in that parish. This is in addition to any regular annual continuing education leave or costs. The sabbatical leave includes continuation of full salary and benefits. The only restriction may be a requirement that the pastor stay with the congregation for at least another year after the sabbatical is completed. Such a program is an excellent way to offer you some intensive time for learning. You and your congregation may be amazed at the improvement in the quality of the sermons after that time is up!

Vacation. Your congregation should not expect you to work seven days a week, fifty-two weeks a year, even if you *do*. Many

Don't ignore your vacation time.

clergy are so conscientious about their ministry and see so much that is not being done and needs doing that they have a hard time taking any time off. But to remain effective in your position, you really need to take a vacation.

Four weeks' vacation is a normal length of time to ask for. But whatever vacation time you receive, be sure that you take it. The congregation won't fall apart during that time. Capable lay leaders can help with the worship and bulletins and cleaning and teaching. It's a good time for people to find out all the things the pastor does, aside from just preaching once a week.

Sample Resolution for Establishment of a Health and Accident Medical Expense Reimbursement Plan

Whereas _____ Church desires to arrange for the payment, directly or indirectly, of medical expenses, to the extent not compensated for by insurance or otherwise, in the event of personal injuries or sickness to _____, his (her) spouse and dependents as defined for Federal income tax purposes up to maximums of 1) $ _____ per year, 2) $ _____ per employee during employment by the Church, 3) $ _____ per spouse and $ _____ per dependent as defined above during related employee's employment by the Church;

And whereas notice of knowledge of this Plan shall be reasonably available to all employees;

And whereas this Plan is established in order that the payments by the above-named Church and the receipts by the above-named employee(s) shall be within the purview of Section 105 of the Internal Revenue Code of 1954 and the United States Treasury Department Regulations thereunder:

Therefore, be it resolved, that the above described plan shall: 1) be and hereby is adopted on behalf of the above-named Church by its Official Board; 2) become effective as of _____ ; 3) continue in effect until terminated by like resolution.

And, therefore, be it further resolved that the Officers of this Church shall be authorized to execute this resolution by all necessary and proper means.

Caveat: Drafting of resolutions should be done by the Church's attorney.

Sick leave. Include sick-leave days in your request for benefits. Pastors do get sick, too. A normal time span for a professional would allow up to two months, with a disability plan taking up salary and housing replacement after that. It is better to have such a plan set forth ahead of time than to have to make decisions under pressure in an emergency.

Day Off. In fairness to yourself and your family, you ought to take a specific day off each week. It won't be Sunday, of course, as it is for other people, and it probably won't be Saturday, either. Find a weekday that is comfortable for you and your congregation and then stick with it. In an emergency, of course, you'll respond on your day off, but normally you won't be available. The arrangement will work out for the church, and your family will appreciate the consideration as well.

R and R on your day off.

Holidays. Pastors should get holidays, too. Do you? Write a few special days into your contract so that they'll be expected as holidays. Perhaps Easter and Christmas are difficult for a pastor to take off, but compensating days can surely be arranged. See if you can find ten or eleven days that suit you. Then, when offered, be sure to take them! After all, if your congregation fails to provide time off for you, you will burn out and the work of the church won't get done very well. In addition, a marriage can quickly suffer when the minister is always "at church."

Scholarships for Children. A special fund for the benefit of the pastor's children to be used toward the costs of college education can be a significant benefit. However, your congregation may have to use some fancy language to get such a plan developed for saving income taxes. The IRS generally will insist that any tuition payments made by the church only on behalf of the children of the congregation's pastor will be taxable income.

Check with your legal counsel to learn about ways in which such a general scholarship fund for the benefit of all children of congregation members might be established, especially for a small amount and to one of the church-related schools.

Malpractice Insurance. If you don't already have a policy of this type, you might want to consider it now. Premiums paid by the church are not taxable income to you. If you do a good deal of counseling, this kind of insurance will be extremely useful if a suit is filed as the result of a bad counseling experience. Some denominations automatically provide malpractice insurance along with the church's general property insurance coverage.

Worker's Compensation. Your state may require your congregation to carry worker's compensation insurance for its employees. Your congregation should carry it anyway to cover the costs of an employee injured on the job. Check with your insurance representative or the state tax office about required coverage. An accident at the church by an employee, including the minister, could be financially disastrous to the employee or the church if this insurance coverage is not available for medical costs, loss of earnings, loss of life, legal defense costs, or judgments.

Unemployment Compensation. Although some nonprofit organizations can elect unemployment insurance coverage if they wish, church organizations usually are not eligible for this coverage. Thus, church workers, including ministers, generally cannot collect any benefits from the government when fired or laid off from their jobs. Of course, no one collects unemployment benefits when he or she voluntarily terminates a job. A severance pay policy, as explained later, would be an important substitute for this coverage.

> Most ministers don't qualify for unemployment compensation.

Club Dues. Generally, dues to professional organizations are a deductible business expense by the pastor. However, dues for local social or service clubs are not deductible unless required as part of the employment agreement. If you belong to a local service club, you may wish to have your congregation pay the dues, especially if you think that your membership benefits the congregation.

Child-care Expenses. By offering to pay for baby-sitters when you and your spouse are expected to attend a church function, the congregation can demonstrate goodwill toward your family. This is financial assistance for a cost that is not normally a deductible business expense. Many employers now provide child-care or day-care expense reimbursement for their employees. You may want to ask for this, too. The tax-free benefit will help stretch your take-home pay. Of course, if you don't get employer reimbursement and both you and your spouse are employed, or one is a student while the other is employed, a child-care tax credit is available.

Other Life Insurance. Because premiums on group term life insurance in excess of $50,000 are taxable income, some congregations wishing to provide more life insurance now pay for other insurance on the life of the minister (sometimes called key person insurance). The church owns the policy, pays the premium, and designates the beneficiary. Premiums paid on a policy controlled by the church are not considered taxable income to the minister. Usually the church designates the pastor's spouse for one-half of the insurance benefit. The key to a tax advantage is that the pastor does not have any ownership or control over the policy. When the pastor leaves, the new congregation may wish to take over the premiums, or the pastor can take them over, or the policy can be cashed in or dropped.

Severance Pay. It is helpful to have a written statement about what you will receive in the event of an involuntary termination of employment. In many places, a paycheck for six weeks' or two months' salary is offered to help the minister meet expenses while searching for other employment.

Maternity/Paternity Leave. A leave of absence at the birth or adoption of a child is appropriate for either mother or father. For women the average leave may be six weeks, for men two weeks. Often pay and benefits will be continued without interruption. It could be another tax-free income benefit to you.

Equity Allowance. If you must live in the church-owned parsonage, you may want to consider asking for an equity allowance. Such an allowance is additional compensation set aside in a special fund that will eventually be available to you for a possible down payment on the purchase of a new home.

The payment into an equity fund is typically equal to the increase in value of the parsonage each year, or it might be a certain percentage of salary. There is no particular tax benefit to you, except for the possible deferment of income taxes on such monies set aside in a tax-sheltered annuity program.

The purpose of a housing equity fund is to help you share with the congregation in some of the increase in the parsonage's equity. An equity allowance (to be distinguished from a housing allowance) certainly can be a great help to a pastor in eventually providing the down payment for a home if and when the parsonage is no longer available.

You can build up equity even in the parsonage. Use an equity allowance.

Housing

The housing arrangement that you have with your congregation is probably the most substantial tax benefit you will enjoy as a pastor. It simply means that the value of the housing provided to you as compensation—a parsonage or a housing allowance—is not subject to income tax. It is excludable, tax-free income. Chapter 6 is entirely about this matter. Read it carefully to learn how you can maximize your housing allowance.

Housing: See Chapter 6.

Salary

Whatever cash salary you receive should be sufficient, adequate, and a fair indication of your worth to the congregation. I hope that your congregation considers your years of experience as well as the size of your congregation when it sets salary. It would be better, however, if they also considered your ability to relate to other people and your skills in handling all of the problem situations that you face every day.

In setting a salary, perhaps a consideration of the wages paid to other professional people would offer some benchmark for what you might be paid. The median salary received by all wage earners in your community would be a good point of comparison. The median salary of the ministers in your denomination also might be helpful.

You will most likely appreciate receiving merit increases in salary as a way for the congregation to say thank you for your good work. Inflation sometimes limits what your congregation will do for you

Adequate pay for a job well done.

above that percentage. Yet, it probably would not be too difficult for your congregation to add the current cost-of-living index to your pay to help you stay even with inflation next year and then to add something extra to tell you that you are appreciated.

Most ministers, if they're paid enough, will stay in their present jobs. It's when salary increases become continually less and less (or even nonexistent) that pastors begin to itch for a change. Some dialog with your lay leaders should help to clarify why a salary increase is or is not given. Needless to say, the more you are paid, the more tax you will pay. Yet no one generally objects to paying more tax on a salary that is fair and adequate.

Pay plans run the gamut; they are not all the same. In developing a pay package that takes advantage of existing tax laws, consider reimbursements first, then benefits, then housing and salary. You can help your lay leaders understand the reason for each element in the compensation package, establish the principle to be applied, consider costs, and then arrange the budget to everyone's satisfaction. Mutual understanding will be critical to development of a successful plan.

2

Budgeting for Family Spending

Like most people, you earn money and then you spend it on the food and shelter and other things that your family needs and wants. You buy life insurance, for example, as a hedge against the time when you may not be around to earn money for the support of those dependent on you. You may buy a car so that you and your family can get around town and go places more conveniently. You and your spouse go out to dinner from time to time, you contribute to your church, and you even spend your money for something frivolous every once in a while. Perhaps you are even able to buy stocks and bonds as investments, if you've saved something.

Needs and wants.

Maybe you spend money first and earn it later, however, which is what may have created your financial problems in the first place. For the purposes of this book, how you spend what you earn is far more important than how you earn it. If earning is a given, then spending must stay within that level of earnings. That's the trick. You must protect your resources and stretch them as far as you can if your earnings are going to be adequate.

That's easily said. But are you:
- ✓ disorganized,
- ✓ procrastinating,
- ✓ "not good at math,"
- ✓ unable to balance the checkbook,
- ✓ not interested in money (!),
- ✓ leaving money matters to your spouse,
- ✓ lazy,
- ✓ too busy?

If any or all of the preceding items apply, making it from one paycheck to the next may be a great challenge. You must learn to manage your money, or you will be in trouble. Is there a solution?

I think that most people do manage their money quite well, and there's no reason to assume that you don't. But if you are having financial difficulties, you must get yourself organized enough to balance your checkbook and you must put your family budget plans at the top of your "to do" list. Procrastinating about money matters is expensive. Not knowing what assets you have or how much you spend

Know your assets and expenses.

23

or what you earn can leave you very uncertain about the future, even from one month to the next.

Use this chapter to help organize your financial life. It doesn't have to become your all-consuming passion, but you will have to make it a priority for awhile, and it does take time.

THE TEN STEPS TO A FAMILY BUDGET

Because extravagant spending is almost always out of the question for a minister's family, prudent management of available resources is important. A sound plan for managing financial resources alleviates worries and allows you and your family to enjoy life more. That brings us to the thrust of this chapter—purposeful personal financial planning for managing your money. This is essential if you are going to maximize the resources you have, secure more resources as needed, and protect the values that you consider important in your life.

For example, you have to eat, of course, but you determine whether you do it frugally or lavishly. You can eat every meal at home and spend less, or you can eat out often and spend more. You can start from scratch in your cooking or use mostly expensive convenience foods. Your choices and your expenses are limited by your goals, preferences, and resources.

Similarly, you need a roof over your head. But not every family is the same size or has the same needs or tastes. An older, larger house may cost more, a small bungalow less. What suits your budget? What is right for your family? Obviously, your available resources determine what you can do. The housing part of your compensation package helps here, too. Knowing your priorities is essential before you can budget for your housing needs.

Budgets don't just appear; they must be carefully planned. After setting goals, you must decide on a time frame for buying and budget (for savings) accordingly. Goals are translated into dollars on your budget, but the dollar amounts may be hard to come by at first. Unless you know how you have been spending your money as well as the things for which you want to spend your money, you can't possibly put a family budget together. You don't have all of the facts. Too many decisions have not yet been made.

Therefore, I like to break down the creation of a family budget into ten steps. Label a file folder or set of folders in which to keep your papers from these ten steps.

Ten steps to a family budget.

1. Record your actual income and expenses for the past year (use Worksheet 1, page 81).
2. List your debts and the amount of your monthly payments.
3. Calculate how much you are worth financially (use Worksheet 2, page 83).
4. Write down your financial goals.
5. List your insurance policies, including annual or monthly premiums (use Worksheet 6, page 91).

6. Show how much you want to save or invest each month.
7. Calculate your estimated monthly income tax and social security tax.
8. Write down your monthly retirement contributions.
9. Plan to set aside funds to build up your estate.
10. Prepare your family budget (use Worksheet 3, page 85).

In the following sections I will comment on each of these steps.

1. Record Your Actual Income and Expenses

If you don't record what you spend your money on, you will never know where all the money goes each month. Most people don't keep any consistent record of how they spend their money, except perhaps a checkbook. The money just comes in and goes out, and when it's gone, a new paycheck will replenish the coffers. This laissez-faire method is certainly undemanding, but it does not allow you to plan for the future or to keep spending under control.

A record system need not be elaborate. Use an 8½- by 11-inch sheet of paper each month. Turn the paper sideways and draw one-inch columns down the short width. Label each column with your most common type of expenditure. (See Worksheet 1 for examples of possible headings for these columns.) Tack the sheet to the refrigerator door.

See Worksheet 1.

Then, every time you or your spouse spend a dime or a dollar, write it down. Record every check you write, not only in your checkbook but also on this sheet. Write down bus fare or the cost of this morning's cup of coffee and roll or the newspaper or whatever you are spending your money on. Yes, it involves a lot of detail, but it's not difficult. The only thing required is remembering to write expenses down. Try it for one month.

Record your expenses.

At the end of the month, total each column and you'll have a rather good record of just how you have spent your money. Multiply the total by twelve, and your estimated annual spending picture will become clearer. Of course, payment for some big-ticket items, such as insurance premiums, occurs only once or twice a year, but you can add 1/12 of that amount to your monthly spending report, if you'd like, to get a feel for how your money is spent or committed each month. With the information you've gathered during the month, complete Worksheet 1 on page 81.

2. List Your Debts and Monthly Payments

In addition to your monthly fixed expenses, be sure that you determine the monthly payments on all your debts. Look at Chapter 3 to get an idea of what you should be doing about what you owe to other people or businesses. List monthly payments on the budget.

List debts.

3. Calculate Your Net Worth

See Worksheet 2. Calculate your net worth.

Knowing what you are worth financially, when compared from year to year, helps you to see how you've been able to manage your resources and how the value of your assets may have grown. It could show reduction in debt, too. Net worth is the difference between your total assets and total debts. It's what you would have left if all your debts were paid off. To find your net worth, complete Worksheet 2 on page 83.

4. Write Down Your Financial Goals

What are your financial goals?

To know where you are headed, write down your financial goals. List what you want to achieve in life financially (or what improved finances can help you to achieve). Goals point you in the right direction; without them, you can easily end up going around in circles.

Perhaps you merely want to stay even—and hope that you can! That's a goal, all right, but you might want to set your sights a little higher than that. Maybe you are spending everything you make. You say that it's necessary spending, and, of course, it may well be. But I challenge you to put aside $25 a month and see if it makes any difference in what you have left over to spend. When you discover that it doesn't (as you will), you can gradually add to that monthly amount. Over a few years, you will discover that you have accumulated a nice nest egg.

Maybe your goal is to amass a substantial amount of savings. Well, that doesn't just happen. You've got to work at it by carefully husbanding your resources, spending no more than necessary and generally being an exceptionally good steward of what you have. A good salary, wise investments, and some careful planning all help you to achieve that goal.

If a trip to Europe is in your thoughts—or at least in your dreams—you'll have some saving to do. Then shop for the best deal. Be flexible about travel dates, and you'll be surprised at the bargains that are available.

Or perhaps you're in desperate need of a new car. Those gravel roads in your country parish or the potholes in the city streets have played havoc with your suspension, and a replacement is needed. If you've read through Chapter 1, you already know that I consider the best route to be for the congregation to own or lease the car you use on church business. If your car is on its last legs, this may be the time to suggest that the congregation buy or lease the new car instead of you.

Plan ahead for big purchases.

Nevertheless, if it's the family car that's falling apart, you'll need to replace it yourself. If you must borrow to buy because you don't have the cash, that is acceptable, but here's a plan to help you avoid a loan and save on interest costs. Once your car loan is paid in four years or so, keep making those payments to yourself for another four years. Then, when the car is eight years old and needs to be replaced, you'll have the cash to do so because you've been paying yourself. You won't need to borrow, and this will save you a great deal of money.

Don't stop there. Keep on putting the equivalent of those old car payments into savings for the next car, if this is possible. Then you may be able to replace the family car in only four years rather than waiting eight long years.

If you still face college costs for your children, you'll need to include those costs in your financial plan as well. Many ministers can't afford to send their children to college, at least not a private or church school. Costs are astronomical and becoming more so—$25,000 a year for the highest-tuition private universities and about $9,000 a year at state schools.

What should you do? First, urge your children to apply themselves in school and get the best marks possible. Students with top grades in high school are sought after by private schools, and with those good grades come scholarships. The best way to assure that college costs will be met is to be certain that your child does everything possible to make good grades that earn generous financial aid.

If your child's grades make the chance of a scholarship unlikely, funding a college education would involve some kind of savings plan. You can set aside $100 a month or more for that purpose. Some colleges allow you to contract with them to fix tuition payments now and make your payments during the years remaining before college begins. You can also buy Series EE U.S. savings bonds (and avoid tax on the interest under current law) as a savings vehicle for college expenses.

Keep in mind that the more you have saved for your child's college education, the less financial aid will be available based on need. Families who have not saved for college but whose children are bright and have potential are likely to secure adequate aid with only limited parental financial help. Considering recent trends involving cutbacks in federal and state financial aid for student loans, I recommend saving for college, but bear in mind that it might work against financial needs assessments.

Of course, when your children apply for college, you will want to explore all possible avenues of financial aid. Because government or private programs change from year to year, you will need to determine the current availability in the year your child is making the application.

You can budget for college expenses in the same way that you budget for a trip to Europe or a new car. Put the money aside in a conservative investment (a money market account at your bank, a money market mutual fund, an income/growth mutual fund, or perhaps even Treasury bills), add to it regularly, and watch it grow. You might talk with your insurance representative about a flexible insurance plan that offers life insurance and investment opportunities in one package (it's a way to build a nest egg while having life insurance in case of your death). These budgeted funds may not pay the entire bill for college, but they will help, and you'll be proud of your financial fortitude.

5. List Insurance Policies and Premiums

List insurance policies and premiums on Worksheet 6.
How much insurance is enough? See Worksheet 5.

Only you can decide how much insurance you really need. Take a look at Chapter 5 on insurance to discover an easy way to figure out how much life insurance you should have. Worksheet 5 on page 89 is helpful. For the moment, just be aware of your monthly premiums for life insurance policies, your homeowner's insurance (or insurance for the furnishings in the parsonage), car insurance, liability insurance, health insurance, and accident and disability insurance. Use Worksheet 6 on page 91 to write those figures down.

6. Determine How Much You Want to Save or Invest

It is essential that you save something. If you don't and there is an emergency or if you live very long past your retirement, you will have nothing to live on. Most likely you'll be at the mercy of your family or your church or some government welfare program. No one wants that, but many people that I know save absolutely nothing. They really do live from one paycheck to the next.

I am going to assume that you would prefer something else, that you really do want to accumulate enough assets to make your retirement living more enjoyable and carefree. That goal is quite possible to achieve when your savings are a top priority. Designate a specific dollar amount on the family budget, then set it aside. It does grow.

Budget for savings.

First save whatever amount you put in the budget. Then, when you've got some accumulation, you may want to invest those savings in something with a little bit better rate of return than a simple savings account. My suggestions for possible ways to invest your extra money are listed in Chapter 4.

You may be saving your money for an immediate purchase or pleasure, but in the long run your most important savings will be for your retirement income. Even though your church pension and social security probably will be substantial, you'll want to supplement that with income from your own investments. Saving while you are young will build the kitty that will provide the extra dollars for fun (or necessities) in retirement.

7. Calculate Your Taxes

Minimize taxes.

There are many ways that you can save on income taxes and social security taxes. Chapter 1 contains some suggestions. My *Tax Planning for Clergy* presents more ideas on what to do. There are many excellent tax guides that you can read to discover new ways to pay less tax. For example, you pay less tax when you make additional contributions to your pension plan or IRAs, when your congregation pays your medical insurance premiums, when you have a medical expense reimbursement plan, when you invest in tax-free municipal bonds (as in a mutual fund, perhaps), when you insist on full reimbursement of professional expenses, when you make charitable contributions for next year this year (itemizing one year, using the standard deduction the other year), when you spend all of your housing allowance but don't overspend it. It's up to you to figure out how much tax you owe. Be sure you know the rules so that you can figure the least possible amount due. The IRS expects no more than that.

8. Calculate Your Monthly Pension Contributions

In retirement, you will need to decide (a) where you are going to live, (b) what you are going to do, and (c) how you will afford to live where you want while doing what you want to do. Retirement income planning then allows you to carry out your decisions.

Plan for retirement.

You probably participate in your denomination's pension plan. That's the best place to put your money now, and it guarantees you a pension income whenever you retire. If you can add to the plan, do so. That will boost your retirement income even more.

The church pension (often designated as housing allowance) and social security may provide only about 70 percent replacement income (at the most) if at least 12 percent of salary plus housing is put in each year for a thirty-five- to forty-year-career. Low-paid pastors will receive a higher percentage or replacement ratio of their last year of income as a social security benefit than will higher-paid ministers. Nevertheless, on average, a 70 percent replacement can be expected for a lifetime of participation in most denominational church pension plans including social security benefits.

If you can add to that your own investment income, you'll have the kind of income you need to continue your present standard of living in retirement. After a few years in retirement, many ministers discover that they have more income than they have ever had before!

9. Review Your Estate Status

As you prepare your family budget, it is important to review your estate status. While the savings line item in your family budget goes to increase your net worth and makes monies available to do what your financial goals call for, it also increases your potential estate. As you review what your estate may amount to someday, you may want to consider the status of your will, any potential estate tax, how you want your assets to be divided, and so forth.

Plan for your estate.

While your estate building may be aimed primarily at developing an adequate retirement income and assets for potential long-term nursing care, nevertheless, you should set forth a plan for distributing whatever is left of your estate at death. The purpose of your will is just that, to tell your survivors how to divide it all up.

Everyone needs a will, even with small amounts of property and life insurance. If there is no will the State decides who gets what.

Be sure you review your will whenever you move, especially to another state, at divorce or death of a spouse, as children grow older, or as new children are born or adopted. Estate planning is an important element of the process of developing your family budget.

10. Prepare Your Family Budget

Use Worksheet 3. Work out your budget.

Finally, your family budget can be put together based on your knowledge of what you are spending now, your goals, and your expectations about what you are able to save. Use Worksheet 3 on page 85 for this purpose. The budget is not merely a long listing of expense items. It is a listing that reflects the many decisions you've made about how you want to spend and save your money.

If you were in financial trouble at the outset of this process, you probably knew that you were spending more than your income, but you didn't know exactly why. With a family budget clearly set forth, you will have these answers. Compare what you expect to spend with what you did spend. Any deviation needs to be evaluated.

Your family budget should be a flexible plan that can be changed as circumstances change. Use your budget to guide your financial decisions and you will soon discover that you not only know how you are spending your money, but that you really are saving money too.

FINANCIAL ADVISORS

Having said all that about managing your own resources (in addition to the advice you will find on investing in Chapter 4), I don't think that you will need to have a professional financial advisor by your side at all times. Nevertheless, a financial advisor could be helpful under certain circumstances.

At its best, financial planning is a comprehensive, impartial, confidential, personalized service that includes estate tax planning, income tax planning, income management, and analysis of investment opportunities (including tax shelter review and recommendations)—all based on the client's particular personal and financial objectives.

These objectives are infinite in their variety and are dependent on individual needs and goals. One person may wish to retire at age 55 with a specific income; another may seek an orderly transfer to children of a business; a third may need only half of current income to live on and wants to shelter the rest from taxation; and so on.

The unique needs and circumstances of the individual and his or her family are the building blocks of a good financial plan. A soundly constructed program depends on the advisor's ability to design a plan that reflects what the client envisages as his or her needs for comfort and security.

How do you find a financial planner to help you sort things out? Because there are so many people involved in financial planning of one sort or another, there are many sources from which you can get service: accountants, tax lawyers, insurance representatives, securities brokers, investment counselors, bankers, and any one of a number of specialists. Generally, all professional financial planners fall into one of two groups: those who charge a fee for their advice and those who charge a fee plus commission. Be aware ahead of time that there is a big difference between these two approaches.

The smallest group includes those planners who charge only a fee no matter what kind of investments you select. They are specialists, however, and like to work mostly with wealthy clients or offer financial counseling to top corporate executives. If you select this type of planner, you should receive a very comprehensive analysis and recommendation report. Although these planners will surely make specific investment recommendations, they sell only their time and expertise.

The other, larger group of planners includes those that operate on a fee-plus-commission basis. Even though they may indeed concentrate on helping you with your financial planning, they are usually trying to sell you something for which they receive a commission. You'll pay a smaller fee for their service than that charged by the fee-only planners, but if you add back the commissions you'd pay, you'll discover that the service is not any less expensive. Objectivity of advice is the issue. Can the person who earns a good commission by selling a specific product be objective in making recommendations to you about investing? Of course you are under no obligation to buy any product from any advisor.

The cost of financial services can range from a low of about $200 up to retainer fees of $20,000 or more. Advisors charging fees within such a wide range of costs will certainly offer varying degrees of expertise and service, and the best advice is not always to be had for the highest price.

Anyone seeking help should shop around to get as many services as possible. Talk to clients of the planners you are considering about the help that they have received. Look in the yellow pages of your telephone book for names of financial advisors. Many are listed. Check with your local library for addresses of national organizations that certify financial planners, and write to them for names of members in your area. Ask your friends.

After you make a selection, you ought to expect the following: an analysis of your income and expenses; a report on the status of your income taxes and various assets; a review of your existing estate plans and recommendations for strategies for your will, trusts, or property transfers; and a program that will help you to reduce your federal and state income taxes.

Total involvement in all aspects of your financial planning, tax reporting, investments, and insurance will make the planner's advice more worthwhile to you. Advisors interested in only selected portions of your financial affairs—just insurance or just investments or just taxes—simply won't be as helpful. Of course, no one can know everything, so your advisor should be able to call upon back-up personnel with legal, accounting, and investment skills.

Ministers need a financial advisor who knows as much as possible about sheltering income from taxes. What income you have must be protected. A skilled financial advisor can do that. Find someone in whom you can trust, a person with integrity, knowledge, and experience—and preferably one who sells only service. You may wish to contact the local consumer credit counseling service, a United Way agency in many communities.

3

Credit Control

How much do you owe? Probably more than you'd like. Most of us find it necessary to use credit occasionally. For family budgeting purposes, what's important is how much you have to pay to others through installment loans, major credit cards, and other charge accounts. You may also still be paying on your school debt, and you probably have a mortgage if you own your own home. Perhaps you make a monthly car payment. For the purpose of this chapter, however, it is the credit card debts that you need to focus on.

Debts.

Those are the debts that you have to pay *now*. Eliminating those high interest-bearing credit card charges is the first priority in bringing your spending down to reality. Undisciplined use of a credit card will make for financial disaster faster than anything else you can do.

DETERMINING YOUR MAXIMUM DEBT LOAD

You probably already have some installment debts that need your constant and regular attention. As you move about in your parish, you'll undoubtedly add to that current listing. You may need to refurnish the parsonage, for example, or to buy a new car or to make some other purchase that you can't put off until future earnings are more secure. Maybe you just don't want to wait any longer, so you go out and buy the item on credit. There is nothing wrong with that as long as you know your limits, you keep your spending under control, and you are sure that you can meet payment commitments.

What is your current debt load? List all of your school, credit card, and personal loans, but do not include mortgages. Then list your monthly payments. Multiply each payment by the number of months that you have left to pay to find the principal and interest. That will be the real cost of the items that you charged. With this listing, you know what to plan for. Use Worksheet 4 on page 87.

Calculate your current debt load.
Use Worksheet 4.

Keep in mind that changes to the Internal Revenue Code are slowly eliminating any Schedule A itemized deduction for consumer interest. By 1991 you won't be able to deduct any of this interest. Charging and not paying the balance due will cost you even more in the future than now. Thus, it is not wise to buy and borrow unnecessarily.

No interest deduction.

There are several rules of thumb to use to determine a safe debt limit. For example, the total of all of your installment debts, some

33

How much debt?

experts say, should be less than 20 percent of your annual take-home pay. (Take-home pay is salary minus taxes and pension.) Another guideline suggests that your total installment debt should not exceed the cash in your savings account. A third says that you should be able to repay all of your installment loans within one year at your current monthly repayment schedule. Finally, some experts say that 10 percent of your monthly take-home pay times eighteen is a safe maximum debt limit.

You'll have to determine what kind of maximum loan limit you are able to carry. Obviously, it is best to have no debt at all, but in our consumer-oriented society, it is difficult to avoid spending for things we think we need or want. Keeping up with the Joneses is indeed a temptation for all of us.

AVOIDING BAD DEBT-MANAGEMENT HABITS

The maximum debt limit that you can safely carry is only one concern. If you don't pay off those loans promptly and properly, you're going to be headed for financial trouble. Here are some danger signals that suggest bad debt-management habits. If these are common to you, you may not have your debt load under control.

1. If you are constantly buying something new without reducing your debt load, you are not managing your finances well. You pay far more for products and services than you realize because of interest and finance charges.

Minimum payments.

2. If you pay only the minimum amount required on your credit card balances each month (the credit card companies love those consumers!), you're treading on thin financial ice. Besides paying a bundle in interest costs, you are not getting out from under that load of debt very fast. In fact, you may not be getting out from under it at all if your minimum payment covers only interest.

3. Some banks provide an automatic loan reserve fund. The purpose of the fund is to loan you money automatically whenever your checking account is overdrawn. It's a convenient arrangement and saves you the hassle and embarrassment of returned checks. But you have to pay off the loan with a specific payment, at interest. The bank generally won't cancel the debt just because you've made a subsequent deposit and your checking account balance is positive once more. Too frequent use of automatic overdrafts is expensive and suggests poor debt management.

New loans for old loans.

4. It's generally not wise to take out new loans to pay off old loans. It may consolidate your debts so that you write one check instead of a dozen, but don't think you suddenly owe less. You may even owe more if the new loan's finance charges are more than the old loan's. If you secured a loan at a high fixed rate of interest and

interest rates have dropped dramatically, refinancing can be advantageous. Don't make it a general practice, however.
5. Skipping required installment loan payments is not smart. Besides prolonging the agony and costing a lot in interest, it has a negative effect on your credit history.

You may need to borrow money. Most of us do. But when you do, remember that it's got to be paid off, and payment should be prompt.

USING CREDIT CARDS WISELY

Please understand me. There is absolutely nothing wrong with using credit cards—I use them all the time. What's wrong is when you pile up debt upon debt plus exorbitant interest costs. The best way to handle your credit card is to use it like cash—paying the balance in full when due.

I never pay any interest charges on my credit cards. If ever the balance on my credit card account begins to accumulate, I will need to dispose of that card. If I don't, that card will ruin me. I use my card a great deal and I delay paying as long as I can, but I always pay the balance and I never pay any interest. I think that it's the best way to use a credit card.

If you do things differently and you know that you cannot pay your bills on time, your first resolution for changing that bad debt-management habit should be to get rid of the credit card without delay, or at least put it away and go without it for awhile. You'll have to work on paying off any balance, of course, but at least you won't be adding anything to it.

Pay on time.

As mentioned previously, if you are accustomed to making only the minimum payments on your Visa or Master Card statements, you are paying a lot extra for any bargains you found. To keep your finances under control, you must not charge more than you can pay off quickly. Avoid finance charges and use your credit card like cash.

Also, avoid a debit card. That's a card that permits you to charge your purchases, just like a credit card, but finance charges begin immediately or your checking account is debited automatically the moment you add a charge. A credit card gives you some days' free use of your money, but a debit card costs you right away. In my opinion, avoid debit cards altogether; write a check or use cash instead.

A debit card.

GETTING OUT OF DEBT—
AND STAYING OUT

As you develop an earnings-savings-spending plan for your family, you must include those payments that you are required to make on your installment loans. We already discussed the budgeting process in Chapter 2. If you can budget to pay debts off in full, fine. In the long run you'll have more spendable money that way.

Any new debt cuts into your available resources for other things that you need or want. This is the trade-off you make when you get a loan or use a credit card because you cannot wait to pay cash. When you borrow money, you have committed future earnings to paying off that debt. Your future disposable income is simply less. This will remain to be true until the loan is paid.

Budget debt payments.

What about the debt you already have? What can you do to get caught up? Quite simply, you must change the way you spend your money. Paying off old debts will require a careful budgeting of your existing and expected resources. You probably will have to spend less so that you can have enough left over to pay those bills. If you have extra income, you could designate that for debt-paying instead of using it to buy something else. If you have life insurance, you could borrow on the cash value, but that money would then not be available in the future. You could borrow from a relative or go to the bank for a loan, but that substitutes one debt for another, which only postpones the problem and doesn't help to solve it.

You could check with a financial advisor on ways to reduce debt, but are there really any other choices than to spend less and pay down the debt? You are still going to have to solve the problem by yourself. Even a financial advisor can't help you there unless you are willing.

If you are really serious about getting out of debt, and staying out, the sensible way is to do the following:

1. Beginning right now, stop using your credit cards. Pay cash or write checks for everything you buy until you have your debt problem under control. Do not incur any new debts.
2. Budget a specific amount, such as $100 a month, to reduce existing debt. Perhaps an automatic withdrawal from your bank account would be helpful to you. You contract with your bank to deduct the specific amount from your checking account on a specific date each month. The bank pays the creditor directly. It's convenient, but you must be sure that you have enough money in the bank to cover the deduction!

Pay on your debt every month.

3. Determine that you *will* spend less on everything. That may mean a reduction in your standard of living. It may also mean foregoing something that you believe to be a necessity.

There is no easy way to pay off debt without giving up something and disciplining yourself to reduce what you owe in a very systematic, deliberate way. A change in your life-style may be necessary to make ends meet. With income lower than most professionals, some ministers may not be able to live as comfortably as they had hoped or as they see other congregation members doing. However, large debts to keep up appearances are not the answer.

Personal debt management is a serious business. How well you manage your own debt will determine to a large degree how well you are able to manage whatever total resources you receive from your congregation.

4

Sensible Investing

I'll always remember the time a minister friend of mine asked me to suggest an investment that would generate a high yield, be completely safe, provide total liquidity, offer the best tax advantage, and be a hedge against inflation—all in one package. I replied, "When you find that one, let me know and we'll both get rich." The animal doesn't exist.

Investing is the process of putting your money to work for you. You do it when you put money in your pension account, fund an IRA, or even buy a house. You may invest in government bonds or certificates of deposit (CDs) in order to earn interest income. When you buy a car so that you can get around town, you are making an investment in your job. When you pay life insurance premiums to build up cash reserves for your family or your own emergencies, you are investing in the future. You also may invest in common stocks to get income from dividends.

Put your money to work.

Many of you may insist that you don't really have any money to invest and that there's not much point in learning anything about it. After all, on a pastor's pay, after groceries, medical bills, car expenses, and all the costs of daily living, how can you have any money left over for investing? As you learned in the chapter on making a family budget, however, saving a small amount each month is an important discipline. And you are probably putting some of your money to work in a pension plan or insurance policy, as noted previously. Before long, it may have built up into an amount large enough to consider investments.

Because buying stocks and bonds is the most common type of voluntary investment, that topic is covered in the second half of this chapter. But before you ever take a flier on the stock market, you need to put your financial house in order on a number of other investment matters.

YOU MUST SAVE MONEY FIRST

Before doing anything else, you'll need a savings plan that forces you to stash something aside regularly for emergencies. You don't dare put your dollars into GM or IBM stock until you've got an emergency savings plan well under way. This fund is to protect yourself from a total wipeout as a result of illness or loss of your job,

Save, now!

to build up funds to make a down payment on a house, or to pay for a college education for your children. In the meantime, the money you're saving certainly can't be kept under the mattress! You'll need a financial instrument that offers safety and liquidity. Here are some good possibilities. Compare and contrast their benefits on Table 1 on page 79.

The familiar passbook savings account offers flexibility, considerable safety, and some return on your money. You can put your money in and take it out anytime. Interest is automatically added to your account regularly. Still, it doesn't offer a very large rate of return—perhaps about 5 percent. A NOW (negotiable order of withdrawal) checking account offers a similar or better rate of return, usually with unlimited check writing privileges. A SuperNOW account does limit withdrawals, but yields are 1 or 2 percent higher. A six-month CD might return 8 percent, depending on the prime interest rate.

Investments beyond these basic savings instruments may carry more risk or tie up your money longer. Your savings account is obviously the place to begin for safety, easy access, and at least some rate of return on your money. Regular deposits will eventually build up into a sizable amount.

When you are ready to invest beyond a mere savings plan, an important point to keep in mind is that you don't dare put your money into any risky investment unless you can afford to lose that money. Your money is safe in a bank or savings and loan association (provided that the institution is insured by an agency of the federal government) or in government securities. Beyond that, there is always a chance of losing what you put into that investment opportunity.

Can you afford to lose your investment?

Investment attitude.

That also raises a question about your own investment attitude. The specific investments you choose may well be determined by your emotional reaction in the face of apparent setbacks or gains. Some people can take a market drop in stride, whereas others panic. Because your investments' value is bound to go up *and* down, your ability to withstand dramatic changes (particularly drops) may determine whether you should really put anything into stocks and bonds.

If you can't afford to lose your money or you become unnerved with a drop in a few points, don't even consider the stock market.

INVESTMENT POSSIBILITIES

If you have adequate savings, you've already launched an investment plan. If you own your own home, you have an investment in real estate. If you collect antiques or stamps or coins, you're not only a collector but also an investor. Insurance, pension plans, social security, and tax shelters are all elements of your investment strategy. Without trying too hard, you may already have done quite well.

Stocks.

Next to a savings account and possibly owning a home, by far the most popular type of investment among ministers is common stocks.

Stocks are easy to buy and sell, and only small sums of money may be required to purchase them. There are, however, other types of securities, many with far less risk than common stocks.

High-grade corporate bonds offer an opportunity for interest income. Unlike shares of stock, bonds eventually mature, and bond holders receive from the company the face value of their securities at that time.

Bonds.

Tax-exempt bonds issued by municipalities also carry specific annual interest income. Because such income is tax free, dollar yields are often less than for corporate bonds. Yet, for taxpayers in a high income bracket, this tax-free yield can be especially important.

A variety of government securities offer the cautious investor a maximum in safety, have generally attractive yields (at least in relation to inflation rates), and are relatively liquid. For example, Treasury bills (T-bills) require a minimum investment of $10,000. Rates vary, but yields are currently around 8 percent. Terms are available for three, six, or twelve months. Since a T-bill is a discount note (interest is paid at the start rather than the end), you'll get a check for your interest within a week of your purchase. Your investment is returned to you at the end of the term. Treasury notes have maturities that range from one to ten years, and bonds have maturities of more than ten years. Treasury bonds often carry quite an attractive long-term yield. Both are available through brokers, banks, or Federal Reserve branch banks.

Government securities.

U.S. savings bonds are now more attractive than ever because the interest rates have increased substantially. Series EE savings bonds are now guaranteed to yield at least 6 percent if held to maturity (generally twelve years). However, because interest is flexible, keyed to the rates paid on other government securities, the yield is currently more. When the interest is received, it is taxable for federal tax purposes. Denominations range from $50 to $10,000.

U.S. savings bonds.

Series HH savings bonds are also available. Converting EE bonds to HH bonds defers payment of income tax on the EE bond interest until the HH bond is redeemed. HH bond interest currently is paid semiannually at about 8½ percent and is fully taxable.

In addition to government securities, there are many varieties of mutual funds that take some of the risks out of investing in individual stocks and bonds. A relatively easy way of investing is to pick a mutual fund that provides the investment vehicle you are looking for, such as a fund that invests only in stocks, only in bonds, or only in government securities. Some funds are combinations whereas other funds specialize in, for example, blue-chip stocks or undervalued stocks or income stocks. No government insurance guarantees your money in a mutual fund, but the return is potentially larger than in less risky government-insured programs.

Mutual funds.

DEVELOP AN INVESTING PLAN AND STICK TO IT!

Regardless of how you want to invest, the development of a plan for investing is of utmost importance. Having such a plan and holding to it is just as crucial to building a sound portfolio as it is to building a good house or creating a successful business. The plan should be based on your financial goals. You may wish to seek competent advice before developing your plan and carrying it out.

Among those investors who do set up a plan, far too many don't stick with it through thick and thin. In periods of heavy optimism (such as 1985 and 1986), they are lured by tips, rumors, greed, and bad advice into speculating when they should be investing. When pessimism prevails (as it did in 1987 and 1988), they end up selling stocks when they should be buying.

Being led astray by emotion can be avoided if the investor first asks some basic questions.

- ✓ How can a sensible plan be constructed?
- ✓ What considerations should be used in selecting suitable holdings?
- ✓ What attitude must be taken when market psychology swings from optimism to pessimism, or vice versa?

Constructing a Sensible Plan

The first point every investor ought to realize is that his or her own investment objective may differ markedly from that of others—the widow next door, a golf partner, one's alma mater, or an employer's retirement fund. A 55-year-old minister whose highly taxed earnings comfortably exceed living expenses obviously does not have the same investment requirements as a church endowment fund that pays no taxes but desperately needs all the current income it can obtain.

Develop your own investing goals.

Thus, every investor—individual and institutional alike—should arrive at a clear understanding of what he or she expects to accomplish with available capital. Is it to be a source of retirement income ten or twenty years hence, or is it to carry the main burden of paying today's bills? Between these two extremes lies an entire range of investment objectives.

The next step is to choose the best means of meeting present needs and reaching future goals. The investor should carefully weigh the pros and cons of fixed-income securities versus common stocks and determine the appropriate mix for a portfolio. Age, temperament, tax bracket, living style, retirement needs, and estate plans must all be taken into account.

Considerations in Choosing Suitable Holdings

Characteristics of companies in which you may want to invest should include: (1) an above average rate of growth, (2) low labor costs, (3) good source of energy and raw materials, (4) availability of retained earnings for funds needed in the future, and (5) pricing flexibility. Companies with those characteristics will be able to withstand the effects of inflation better than most other companies.

The Importance of a Stable Investment Attitude

The great majority of the nation's shareholders—and an even larger portion of those unacquainted with investing—believe that the high road to investment success is through "buying low and selling high" and repeating the process over and over. In this way of thinking, a stock is nothing more than a piece of paper on which to make an easy profit when and if it goes up. Under current tax law that profit is taxed at the same rate as income. However, Congress is expected to reintroduce a tax advantage for profit from the sale of property.

Buy low, sell high is not a realistic goal—consistently.

The wide publicity given to price fluctuations, to short-term changes in earnings, to temporary but insignificant new developments, and to the shifting of big chunks of money from one issue to another by investment institutions all tend to create the impression that the stock market is just an enormous casino rather than a genuine auction of capital assets. "Yet what happens in the securities markets at each major downturn," says David L. Babson, investment counselor, "should make it obvious that the buy-low, sell-high philosophy is a cruel myth. When attempted repeatedly, it is bound to produce poor—even disastrous—results, because it requires a combination of shrewdness, courage, independence, timing and luck that no human being can hope to experience consistently.

"The vital fact to be borne in mind is that building up one's assets is a project that usually covers a period of many years. If the stocks selected are those of strong, expanding companies, history shows that the rewards of investment in their long-term progress will be surprisingly large in the end.

"Just as importantly," says Babson, "the investor should not panic during bear markets and sell out. The shareholder of fundamentally sound companies can look upon a drop in the price of a good stock not as a catastrophe but as an opportunity to buy more. In contrast, at such times the owner of shares in a 'turnaround' or 'special situation' usually becomes frightened and either sells outright at the bottom or as soon as a small part of a huge loss can be recovered.

"The investor should continue to invest surplus income as it becomes available—if possible, as regularly and periodically as insurance premiums are paid. By so doing, the investor will continually be building up a portfolio base and will be much less likely to become sidetracked from the original goal by shifts in market psychology.

Regular investing.

"If new cash is regularly added to a fund, and if properly qualified stocks are purchased, the investor will have secured holdings at fair average prices. What these securities may do price-wise in a week or a month or even the next few years after their purchase is not the main issue. The true test of the soundness of those selections will be how much their earnings and dividends have increased after five or ten years.

"Sticking to this long-range program can also prevent the investor from making another common type of error—selling a suitable stock because its earnings suffer a quarterly drop or because it runs into one of the slow periods that occur for even the best-managed companies. Having a plan gives the investor the patience to hold on to the right stocks even during their recurring periods of unpopularity.

"Over a period of years, the long-term investment characteristics of a company or industry may deteriorate. So the investor should be alert to changes and be willing to weed out holdings where the fundamentals no longer measure up in favor of others where the basic situation has improved.

"Building a well-balanced portfolio that fits the investor's needs and objectives seems like a simple task. Actually, it is quite difficult, because it requires great self-discipline to continue with the program originally laid down, and it calls for a more coldblooded attitude towards one's capital than most people can muster.

"In summary," says Babson, "the investor who bases an approach to investing on holding a part-ownership in companies with favorable investment characteristics is following a sensible long-range plan. This is a proven strategy which is certain to produce good results over a period of years."[1]

REVIEW YOUR PLAN FREQUENTLY

No matter what your investment strategy may be, the decisions that you've made are certainly not the last word. Regular review and updating, as necessary, is important on every one of your investments. Circumstances change, sometimes drastically and in short order, and you can't afford to let things lie idle or unattended. Thus, persistent concern and attention to the investments in which you've put your money is essential.

Investments in stocks and bonds bear close watching all the time. But, as mentioned previously, a drastic drop in the Dow-Jones average is not necessarily cause to dump your portfolio. The basic strength of the securities that you own is important. You'll want professional advice before making changes.

Even your church pension-plan investments, insurance, and social security should be reviewed regularly. You ought to know what your pension plan's board of directors is doing with your investments. Your insurance needs change as your income and family situation

---

[1] David L. Babson, *The Babson Staff Letter*, David L. Babson & Co. Inc., One Boston Place, Boston, Mass.

change over the years, and coverage should be adjusted accordingly. And although there's not much you can do about social security, be sure that your account is getting credited for your annual contribution. You also ought to keep abreast of what your benefits are expected to be.

5

Insurance for Ministers

Some ministers, believing that they cannot afford the cost of insurance, have none. Other ministers carry so much insurance as to be what is termed "insurance poor"—they pay too much compared with the benefit provided. Yet in today's society, no minister's family can afford to be without health, disability, or life insurance, in spite of the cost.

Insurance is required to maintain a responsible financial life. Its purpose, of course, is to protect the insured against financial disaster upon the occurrence of a financial casualty that exceeds the insured's available resources. Few ministers could afford to shell out $50,000 for a medical emergency, for example, yet that amount is not uncommon. A surviving spouse could not easily replace the earnings of the minister spouse upon death, especially when there are small children at home. A successful liability suit for a million dollars would forever relieve a minister of all assets.

Health insurance, a necessity.

Fortunately, most denominations now provide needed health and disability insurance coverage as well as survivor's benefits. The costs for these benefits (usually quite high—perhaps as much as 25 percent of salary) are paid by the congregation. When congregations do not or cannot provide such coverages, however, the minister should promptly secure the coverage. One cannot afford to be without it.

There are many types of insurance. This chapter describes several kinds of casualty insurance and life insurance. When purchasing casualty insurance, you are securing protection for an unknown loss; when purchasing life insurance, you are providing protection against a known loss, although the time of its occurrence is uncertain. Casualty insurance provides protection for loss of property and illness, items over which we have no control. Life insurance is meant to replace income lost because of the insured's death. Sometimes life insurance is also purchased to build up cash reserves for emergencies or to generate investment income.

CASUALTY INSURANCE

Two principles generally govern the amount of casualty insurance needed: the large-loss principle, and the first-dollar principle.

According to the large-loss principle, a policy is purchased to insure against the largest possible loss that might be incurred in a disaster. The object is to protect oneself from having to use current resources to pay for a very large loss. A major medical health insurance policy is of this type. Its purpose is to pay for potentially large medical expenses that an individual could never personally afford.

The first-dollar principle assumes that one may be willing to pay for the costs of small losses. If you lose a car hubcap, for example, you can afford to pay for the replacement. If you bought insurance against such a loss, it would cost you far more than the value you might ever possibly receive. That's why you pay for the first-dollar costs when you go into the hospital or have a fire. The deductibles on your policies are the self-insurance part of your protection plan. To hold down insurance premium costs, participants pay their own first-dollar losses and then expect the insurance company to pay for the big losses.

First dollar, large-loss principles.

Health and Disability Insurance

Illness and accident and the subsequent loss of income are among the hazards of life. Every minister's family needs a good health insurance plan to protect the family members from the high cost of being sick or disabled. An inadequate health insurance plan may need to be supplemented with another policy. When a minister is anticipating retirement, a policy that guarantees lifetime coverage (as is provided by most church plans) will be important.

Some health insurance policies divide major medical and basic coverages; others include all coverages in one plan. If you have a choice, you certainly want the major medical aspect, if possible without any upper limit. Such a policy will pay for the really big medical costs. In addition, a basic plan will pay for much of the deductible of the major medical plan. If you cannot afford to pay large deductible amounts yourself, a basic plan will be desirable. Yet even then there is a deductible; you will always pay some of the first-dollar costs of any illness.

Health insurance plans also provide coinsurance features. That means that you may have to pay, for example, 20 percent of a loss up to a specific amount while the plan pays for 80 percent of the costs. After a limit is reached, the plan pays 100 percent of the costs.

Coinsurance.

A coordination-of-benefits clause (included in virtually all church health insurance plans) provides for coordination of the payment of benefits between two or more insurance companies with whom you may have policies. If you have two group health insurance policies, for example, you cannot collect more from both policies than the total costs you incurred. One policy will be primary and pay all appropriate benefits; the other plan will pay what it would have paid, reduced by what the first plan has paid.

Coordination of benefits.

Your health insurance policy will cover a variety of medical costs. If you have to shop around for a policy, it is important to compare coverages. Lower premiums do not necessarily mean better coverage. Please keep in mind that no church's health insurance policy covers every possible illness or condition; to do so would be prohibitively expensive. Be sure that you know what is and what is not covered in your policy so that you will not be surprised when a claim is made.

Also be aware that the premium you pay for your church health insurance coverage is directly related to the benefits that are paid out to all participants. The more coverage provided, the greater the premium expense. Thus, some extremely expensive medical procedures are not covered in church plans because even one case would raise all premiums significantly.

Disability insurance. Disability or loss-of-income policies are often considered to be part of health insurance coverage. To lose your job because of illness or accident can be financially disastrous. Ministers should be certain that they are adequately covered. In addition to disability benefits provided by a church plan, social security offers disability benefits after five months of total and presumably permanent disability. Additional disability coverage beyond the church plan and social security is probably not necessary. A disability income-replacement value of about two-thirds of your previous income (assuming adequate health insurance) is probably adequate for you to maintain your standard of living.

Many congregations will continue salary and housing to a minister for a period of time during a long illness. You should not expect much beyond three months and perhaps nothing after six months. Careful planning in advance will help you to avoid a potentially bad situation.

Property and Liability Insurance

Ministers are faced not only with the perils of illness, accident, and loss of income but also with loss or damage to their property and the possibility of being sued. Because one cannot possibly insure against all potential risks, it is important to determine the greater risks and insure them first.

Homeowner's policy. Ministers who own or drive an automobile should have adequate insurance against collision, liabilities to property and persons, and other perils as needed. Many ministers own their own homes, and most ministers own their own household furnishings. Homeowners will certainly carry a basic homeowner's policy for loss against fire and other perils to a house and its contents. Ministers who live in parsonages need the same basic type of policy to cover their household goods. If there is a loan against a property, the lender will require adequate insurance coverage. In addition, ministers should be certain that their personal libraries are adequately covered, whether located at home or in the church office.

Protection against the risks of being sued is important. Even though you think that you don't have anything of value that could be used to pay off such a claim, you probably do (check your net worth statement developed in Chapter 2 again). Liability coverage is essential. (Malpractice insurance was briefly discussed in Chapter 1.)

Life Insurance

The purpose of any life insurance policy is to provide a sum of money that can be used to pay for some large expense or be invested to replace income lost because of death of the insured. The benefit is for those dependent on that lost income. Life insurance has no deductible.

Basic features of typical varieties of life insurance are listed in the table on page 48.

To determine whether you may need additional life insurance, ask yourself these questions:

1. What assets do I already have, including life insurance, that can be invested to earn an income?
2. What are the lump-sum cash needs, such as burial costs and an emergency fund, that my family might need at my death?
3. How much income do I need to provide for my family after social security and church pension funds are considered?
4. What additional sum of money do I need to make available at my death that will provide sufficient income for my family when invested?

Use Worksheet 5 on page 89 to make your calculation of estimated insurance needs on the life of the principal money earner in the family. That's not all the insurance you may want to consider, however.

Use Worksheet 5. Calculate your insurance needs.

What about life insurance for your spouse? If the employed spouse is the survivor and the other spouse has been at home taking care of small children, don't fool yourself into thinking that everything stays the same financially after that spouse's death just because income has not disappeared. The death of a spouse who had not been employed may not decrease income, but it will almost certainly increase costs. A life insurance policy on the spouse is desirable to cover those potential future costs.

What about life insurance for children? Although parents would seldom suffer any loss of income or support from the death of a minor child, there are funeral costs and perhaps other final costs. Sometimes juvenile insurance policies are purchased by parents to guarantee coverage for their children when the children are older and need the coverage but, because of a health problem then, may not be able to purchase any. Generally, though, life insurance on children is not a top priority. Adequate coverage for the wage-earning spouse is the most important consideration.

Life insurance for children.

Life Insurance Compared

Term Insurance
1. Provides the greatest amount of coverage for the least amount of cost for younger people. Becomes prohibitively expensive at older ages.
2. Pure life insurance. Pays only at death of insured.
3. Has no cash or loan value.
4. Level premiums, decreasing coverage; or level coverage, increasing premiums.

Permanent Insurance
1. Fixed policy amount that pays at death of insured.
2. Accumulates a cash value that can be borrowed or paid when policy is cashed in, such as at retirement.
3. Fixed premium amount.
4. More expensive than term, especially for younger people.
5. Available for a lifetime, or available for a limited pay life specific time, although at higher cost.

Endowment Insurance
1. Most expensive of all life insurance.
2. Forced savings plan, but with low interest rate.
3. Cash reserve of policy face value payable at specific age or life insurance value paid at death of insured.

Flexible Insurance
1. Combines life insurance with investments.
2. Flexible face value of policy; flexible amount designated for investment.
3. Flexible premiums based on insurance needs and investment objectives.
4. Usually eliminates additional physical when face value is increased.
5. May provide a cost-of-living option.

Of course, life insurance can be used to accumulate funds for some future event or need, such as a college education. An endowment policy is often used for that purpose. At the end of the term or upon the death of the insured, the money promised will be available.

If you borrow money, you may have to provide life insurance to cover the balance of the loan in case of your death. Sometimes called "mortgage insurance," it is most often used in connection with the purchase of a home. The premiums become part of the monthly mortgage payment, and the bank or lending institution becomes the beneficiary.

There are various types of life insurance policies, yet all insurance policies are basically either term insurance or permanent (whole life) insurance.

Term Insurance

Term insurance offers the greatest coverage for the least amount of money. It is pure life insurance, nothing else.

Term insurance may carry either a level or an increasing annual premium amount. It can have a constant or a decreasing face value as the purchaser grows older. Thus, you can buy a $20,000 policy, for example, and pay a higher rate each year, or you can pay the same premium each year and have less coverage each year. There are variations. With a five-year or ten-year renewable term policy, a level policy amount is usually maintained for five or ten years but an increasing premium rate is charged either each year or when the policy amount changes. In most cases, such a policy can be converted to permanent life insurance without further proof of insurability. A given amount of permanent insurance coverage will be considerably more expensive than the same amount of term insurance. Unlike term insurance, however, permanent insurance does build a cash reserve.

Inexpensive insurance for young people.

Permanent Insurance

Permanent (or whole life) insurance is another variety of life insurance. Two forms are straight life and limited-payment life. Premiums are generally paid for life on a straight life policy (hence are lower). With limited-payment life, the policy specifies exactly how long premiums must be paid; after that time the policy is paid up, and no more premiums are due. In all permanent insurance policies, a cash value is accumulated eventually.

Permanent insurance, therefore, differs from term insurance in that the permanent policy costs more, builds up a cash reserve, maintains a level policy amount and premium, and pays exactly the face amount of the policy at death.

Permanent insurance also offers the purchaser the opportunity to borrow the cash value at lower interest rates than those charged by most lenders. Some older policies charge only 5 or 6 percent interest. That is cheap money. Also, there is no requirement to pay back the money at any time—only payment of interest is required. Any loan balance at death is simply deducted from the proceeds paid to the designated beneficiary.

The cash value of permanent insurance generally is used in only two ways: (1) it can be borrowed, or (2) it can be collected if the

Cash value life insurance.

policy is cashed in. Yet a permanent insurance policy is not a good investment vehicle, because the cash value is less than the premiums paid, and the face amount of the policy will be paid anyway. If you are looking for a prudent way to increase your net worth, it is best to consider other investment means.

Endowment Life Insurance

An endowment life insurance policy can be quite expensive. Some persons believe that it can be useful in accumulating a guaranteed sum at a specific time for the insured or in providing the same amount of money at the death of the insured prior to the policy's due date. It is indeed a forced savings plan, but the rate of return may be as low as 5 percent. The emphasis is on building a cash reserve that endows at a specific age and, in the meantime, having life insurance coverage of the same amount.

Flexible Policies—Universal Life or Adjustable Life

The insurance companies have not been idle in recent years as interest rates have soared and people have sought alternative investment vehicles. To encourage more people to buy life insurance and invest their money with the insurance company at the same time, flexible policies have been devised. Most of these come under the heading of universal life or adjustable life policies.

Universal life.

These policies give policyholders an opportunity to change their minds about how much life insurance they want to buy and how much they want to invest. Premiums on a flexible policy can be raised or lowered to fit individual budget needs. A guaranteed increase option agreement provides an opportunity for raising or lowering coverages. As insurance needs (or investment needs) change, such as at the birth of another child or on receipt of a pay raise that gives the purchaser more to invest, that individual is allowed to change the premium, the policy amount, or the amount invested.

A flexible policy eliminates the need to choose among various life insurance programs. Decisions can easily be made about the coverage desired and the additional premium to be invested. It is not necessary, therefore, to buy a new policy and seek a new physical examination every time face amounts or investment objectives change. (However, a substantial increase in coverage may be available only upon proof of satisfactory health.)

A Precautionary Note

Even if you feel that you are down to your bottom dollar with no immediate prospect of a cash advance on next month's salary, don't ignore your health, disability, liability, and life insurance needs.

Ideally, the congregation should pay for this expense as an employee benefit, but some won't. If you think that you can't meet the payments, request help from the congregation anyway. Check with your denominational pension board and ask for assistance in meeting any premiums. You simply cannot afford to be without coverage.

6

Housing for Ministers

There is absolutely no better way for a minister to reduce tax liability and save money than by maximizing the use of Section 107 of the Internal Revenue Code dealing with the value of housing provided by the congregation.

The law is simple and to the point. The value of the parsonage and utilities provided to the minister is not reported as taxable income for income tax purposes. And the amount of housing allowance paid to a minister is not taxable for income tax purposes to the extent spent or used to provide a home. (The values are taxable for social security tax purposes.)

No income tax on clergy housing values.

Some creative use of the housing allowance, whether you own your own home or live in the parsonage, can increase your take-home pay. With proper planning, your church pension designated as housing allowance can also increase your retirement income. If you understand the tax laws and fully take advantage of them, you will certainly be able to make your paycheck go further.

UNDERSTANDING THE LAW

Section 107 of the 1954 Internal Revenue Code (revised) is simple, easy to understand, short, and to the point. It reads:

> In the case of a minister of the gospel, gross income does not include: 1) the rental value of a home furnished to him [sic] as part of his compensation; or 2) the rental allowance paid to him as part of his compensation, to the extent used by him to rent or provide a home.

Religious functions.

Not everyone who calls himself or herself a minister or even who is ordained may necessarily take advantage of Section 107. The regulations specify that in order to qualify for the exclusion, the home or rental allowance must be provided as remuneration for services that are ordinarily the duties of a minister of the gospel. Examples of specific services cited in the regulations, the performance of which will be considered duties of a minister of the gospel for purposes of Section 107, include "the performance of sacerdotal functions, the conduct of religious worship, the administration and maintenance of religious organizations and their integral agencies, and the performance of teaching and administrative duties at theological seminaries."

The regulations further state that Section 107 is applicable only to duly ordained, commissioned, or licensed ministers of churches.

Furthermore, whether the service performed by a minister is really in the conduct of religious worship or the ministration of sacerdotal functions depends on the tenets and practices of the particular church or church denomination. Service performed by a minister in the exercise of ministry must be under the authority of a religious body constituting a church or church denomination.

Thus, the term "minister of the gospel" for purposes of Section 107 means an individual who is duly ordained, commissioned, or licensed to the pastoral ministry by action of a religious body constituting a church or church denomination and who is invested with the authority to conduct religious worship, to perform sacerdotal functions, and to administer ordinances or sacraments in accordance with the prescribed tenets and practices of such church or church denomination.

In cases in which a church or church denomination ordains some ministers of the gospel and licenses or commissions other ministers, the licensing or commissioning of an individual as a minister of the gospel must establish a status that is the equivalent of ordination and is so recognized by the church. That is, the individual, upon being licensed or commissioned, must be invested with the status and authority of an ordained minister, fully qualified to exercise substantially all of the ecclesiastical duties of such a minister in that denomination.

Thus, services rendered by an individual minister in the conduct of religious worship or the ministration of sacerdotal functions are considered to be services in the exercise of ministry whether or not such services are performed for a religious organization or an integral agency thereof. Such religious activities, however, must be in accordance with the tenets and practices of a particular religious body constituting a church or church denomination.

Services rendered by an ordained minister of the gospel who is employed as a teacher or administrator are considered duties of a minister of the gospel only when such services are rendered for an organization that is an integral agency under the authority of a religious body constituting a church or church denomination.

Ministers who perform services pursuant to an assignment or designation by their church are considered ministers of the gospel even though the services are not being performed for an integral agency under the authority of that church.

Teachers.

Ordained ministers who perform teaching and administrative duties at theological seminaries are considered ministers of the gospel for purposes of Section 107 only if the seminary is an integral agency of the church or if the minister was assigned by the church to perform that duty.

DETERMINING THE HOUSING ALLOWANCE

The amount of possible housing allowance varies according to each pastor's circumstances, as does the amount of housing allowance that can be excluded from taxable income. The two amounts are not necessarily the same, even for the same pastor. Here's why.

The general rule is this: The amount of housing allowance that a pastor receives in any one year cannot exceed the fair rental value of the home in which the pastor lives, furnished, plus the cost of utilities. Furthermore, the amount of housing allowance that can be excluded from taxable income cannot exceed (1) the allowance itself, (2) the amount actually used "to provide a home," or (3) the fair rental value, whichever is lower. Therefore, the amount of housing allowance any particular pastor will need depends on how much that pastor expects to spend "to provide a home." Regardless of what the pastor expects to spend, the amount of the housing allowance cannot exceed the fair rental value of the home, furnished, including the cost of utilities.

Fair rental value is maximum housing allowance.

Any amounts spent in excess of the allowance are not excludable; any allowance not used is taxable income and is reported as "other income" on Form 1040. Thus it is generally best to have the maximum amount of housing allowance designated even if it may not all be used.

Pastor determines amount of allowance.

Many congregations review their pastor's compensation, including the provision for housing, each year (as they should). But the congregation should not tell the pastor how much of his or her compensation will be for a housing allowance. It may be less than that permitted by the IRS and may not be enough to cover the pastor's expenses, thus depriving the pastor of a potential income exclusion. The pastor should ask the congregation to set a total amount for salary and housing combined. Then the pastor should be allowed to suggest how much should be designated for housing, depending on his or her personal circumstances.

With a housing allowance, a pastor can pick and choose any house that fits the needs and tastes of the family. After all, it's not the congregation's house; it's the pastor's home for that family, bought or rented to satisfy their requirements. It can be a Victorian manse or a tiny bungalow, an apartment in the city, or a big house in the country. One purpose of an allowance is to give the pastor the freedom to make a personal choice. And that choice may require more or less than what the congregation thinks the pastor should spend for housing.

According to the IRS and the general rule stated previously, the amount of the housing allowance has to do with the rental value of the home selected and the amount spent to provide a home. It should be determined by what the pastor *has* done rather than what the members *think* should be done.

Let's consider an example. Assume that lay leaders in a congregation insist that $5,000 a year is sufficient to provide the kind of house that their pastor "should" live in. A $5,000 allowance plus $15,000 salary is designated, for a total annual payment of $20,000. The pastor should be able to advise the lay leaders of the congregation on how much of that $20,000 income is to be designated as housing allowance. If the pastor can justify $7,000 under the rules, then by no means should the congregation say it cannot be done, that $5,000 is all it will allow. To limit the allowance to the lower figure could cost the pastor $300 in additional income tax (assuming a 15 percent tax bracket times $2,000).

In this example, then, as long as the rental value of the pastor's furnished home and the cost of utilities do not exceed $7,000, the amount is quite proper. Housing allowance is officially designated as $7,000 and cash salary as $13,000.

The pastor then must keep careful records to justify the exclusion of the allowance from taxable income. Only what is spent is excludable. On the one hand, if $5,500 is spent to provide housing—mortgage payments, taxes, furnishings, repairs, utilities, and all the other costs—the pastor may exclude $5,500 of that $20,000 salary from taxable income. The rest, $14,500, is taxable income. On the other hand, if $7,500 happens to be spent to provide housing, only $7,000 can be excluded, and $13,000 of income is subject to tax.

Exclude expenditures only up to rental value.

In any event, if the original $5,000 allowance had been required, the pastor would have overspent either way and, being unable to deduct that excess, would have been penalized by the congregation by having to pay more income tax than was necessary.

Of course, a housing allowance can be used only "to provide a home" for qualifying ministers. Thus, no part of an allowance can be used for the costs of housing not used by the minister as a principal residence. In the case of a duplex, for example, the minister may use the allowance only for those costs that apply to the half the pastor's family lives in. Costs that cannot be specifically identified, such as insurance or taxes or mortgage payments, should be divided in half if both sides are substantially the same size; otherwise they should be divided in proportion to square footage. Costs and income associated with the rental side of the duplex are treated the same as for any kind of rental property.

A housing allowance cannot be used to pay for a vacation home or a future retirement home while the minister is living in the parsonage. It is, of course, commendable to plan for retirement housing, but the housing allowance can be used only for expenses to provide a home that is the principal residence of the pastor. When a parsonage is provided and lived in by the pastor's family, even if only part of the time, the parsonage is assumed to be the principal place of residence. Any housing allowance paid to the pastor in that case would be appropriately used only for expenses to provide a home in the parsonage.

A second home.

RENTAL VALUE CALCULATION

Ministers living in a church-owned house as well as those receiving a housing allowance must estimate the rental value of the homes in which they live.

The most acceptable way to determine rental value is by securing an appraisal from a real estate person qualified to make such appraisals. The IRS may insist on an appraisal if the original estimate appears to be inaccurate. Rental values can often be easily determined simply by asking a real estate friend for an opinion or by finding out what typical rents paid for similar housing in the neighborhood are.

How to figure fair rental value.

A popular rule of thumb suggests that a reasonably accurate guess can be made by using a monthly figure equal to 1 percent of the fair market value of the home. Thus, a $60,000 home might rent, unfurnished, for $600 a month. The rule of thumb may not always be applicable, however, and the reasonableness of an estimate will have to be reviewed. A $125,000 home, for example, may not rent for $1,250 a month. A lower figure may be more accurate.

For those ministers who receive a housing allowance, the allowance need not be limited to just the rental value of the unfurnished home. According to the IRS, the maximum housing allowance may also include a rental value on furnishings. Thus, a pastor in a $60,000

A furnishings allowance.

personal residence with $10,000 worth of furnishings and $2,400 a year in utility costs may be able to secure a $10,000 annual housing allowance ($60,000 times 1 percent per month plus $10,000 times 1 percent per month plus $2,400). The allowance is excludable from taxable income to the extent used. For those who live in a parsonage and who furnish the home on their own, the 1 percent rule is generally acceptable for the rental value of furnishings.

It should be noted that the fair rental value of the parsonage, manse, or rectory is included in income subject to the social security self-employment tax (as is any housing allowance received).

PROCEDURES FOR ESTABLISHING A HOUSING ALLOWANCE

Procedures.

Proper designation of an allowance in advance of its use is required in order to qualify for the exclusion. Three documents are generally used to verify proper action by the official board of the congregation prior to the payment of any allowance.

First, the minister should submit a request for a housing allowance, such as the sample on page 57.

Second, the official board should record its action of designating the housing allowance in its official minutes. A sample is provided on page 57.

Minister's Estimate of Rental Value

To: Name of church or organization
From: The Rev. _____
Subject: Parsonage allowance for 19____

I request a housing allowance of $ _____ for 19____.
The estimated fair rental value of my home furnished, plus the cost of utilities, is $ _____. My request does not exceed the fair rental value.

Date: _____

_____
Minister's signature

Insert for Minutes of Meeting

The chairperson informed the meeting that under the tax law, an ordained minister (1) is not subject to federal income tax with respect to the parsonage allowance paid to him/her "as part of compensation to the extent used to rent or provide a home" and (2) is not subject to federal income tax on the rental value of a home supplied to him/her rent-free.

The board on the ____ day of _____, 19____, after considering the statement dated _____ from the Rev. _____ setting forth the amount the Rev. _____ estimates to be the fair rental value of the home, furnished, plus the cost of utilities, on motion duly made and seconded, adopted the following resolution:

Resolved, that the Rev. _____ receive compensation of $ ____ of which $ ____ shall be designated a parsonage allowance. (If the minister is to have the rent-free use of a home, also state: The Rev. _____ shall also have the rent-free use of the home located at _____ for the year 19____ and for every year thereafter as long as the Rev. _____ is pastor of this congregation.) The parsonage allowance (and rent-free use of a home) shall be so designated in the official church records.

Third, the secretary of the official board should inform the minister of the action taken and the amount of the allowance as in the sample provided below.

Notification by Employer

Date: _____

Dear _____:

This is to advise you that at a meeting of the committee held on _____, your parsonage allowance for the year 19___ was officially designated and fixed in the amount of $ _____. Accordingly, $ _____ of the total payments to you during the year 19___ will constitute parsonage allowance, and the balance will constitute compensation. Under Section 107 of the Internal Revenue Code, an ordained minister of the gospel is allowed to exclude from gross income the parsonage allowance paid as part of compensation to the extent used to rent or provide a home. You should keep an accurate record of your expenditures to rent or provide a home in order to be able to substantiate any amounts excluded from gross income in filing your federal income tax return.

Sincerely,

_____
Secretary of the Board

HOW TO USE THE HOUSING ALLOWANCE

A housing allowance may be used for all expenditures required to provide a home, with the exception of the cost of food and maid service. Thus, the allowance may be used for the down payment on the purchase of a home, real estate taxes, mortgage payments, interest, insurance, repairs, utilities, furniture, furnishings, yard care, and so on. Unused allowance is taxable income. Amounts spent in excess of the designated allowance are not deductible.

The only way that a housing allowance can be excluded from taxable income is by spending it "to provide a home." And perhaps the largest single item for which an allowance is used is for mortgage payments. If the mortgage is paid off, however, the housing allowance is no longer being spent for that purpose. In that case, nothing is excludable for housing payments or rental value except what is actually spent to provide a home (i.e., utilities, repairs, insurance, and so on). That means that pastors who are paying on a mortgage pay less income tax, all else being equal, than those who have had the foresight, fortitude, discipline, and ability to pay off their mortgages. The housing allowance rules do indeed encourage pastors to carry a home mortgage debt into retirement.

Allowance must be spent to be excludable.

To maintain the favorable exclusion available when making mortgage payments, some clergy have refinanced their homes after the mortgage was paid off in order to use more of their housing allowances. Money received from that refinancing has gone for down payments on a second home, into savings, or perhaps into securities. The loan was not secured to provide a home, yet the mortgage payments are now purportedly counted as a use of the housing allowance. I don't think that such an arrangement would be approved by the IRS upon audit because the loan payments are not being made "to provide a home." The refinancing route is probably best avoided.

Refinancing a mortgage.

Clergy homeowners may continue to deduct mortgage interest and real estate taxes on Schedule A even though such expenses were paid for out of the excludable housing allowance. (Rev. Rul. 83-3, which had denied this "double" tax benefit, was repealed retroactively by the 1986 Tax Reform Act.)

IF YOU LIVE IN A PARSONAGE

Unfortunately, there is no tax-code section, regulation, revenue ruling, or court case that specifically says that for pastors in a parsonage, a furnishings allowance may be designated and excluded from taxable income to the extent used. Nevertheless, the designation of a rental allowance to ministers who also receive the rent-free use of a parsonage is appropriate. And to the extent that it is used for furnishings and other expenses required to provide a home, that allowance is excludable from taxable income.

The tax-savings significance of this kind of designation can be dramatically illustrated. Assume that a minister receives a $15,000 salary with an unfurnished parsonage provided and all utilities paid by the congregation. Assume further that the minister expects to spend $1,000 during the year for additional furniture, some drapes, minor repairs to the front steps, grass seed, and a new television, none of which will be reimbursed by the congregation. If no allowance is designated, the minister has $15,000 of income subject to tax. On the other hand, if salary can be reduced to $14,000 and a $1,000 rental allowance designated, then, to the extent used, that $1,000 may be excluded from taxable income. For a minister in the 15

A furnishings allowance in the parsonage.

percent tax bracket, that simple designation will save the pastor's family $150 in income tax. A congregation can actually boost its pastor's take-home pay by $150 in this way, and it will cost the congregation nothing at all.

Pastors in unfurnished parsonages may receive a supplemental furnishings allowance that may be used to purchase furniture, furnishings, yard care, and repairs and to cover other costs not otherwise provided by the congregation. A furnishings allowance may not exceed the difference between the fair rental value of the parsonage furnished and unfurnished. A designated payment may be provided by the congregation for the allowance, or salary can be reduced by the allowance amount. The allowance is excludable from taxable income to the extent that it is spent. Unspent allowance is taxable income; any overexpenditure is not deductible, just as for any housing allowance.

HOW TO REPORT THE HOUSING ALLOWANCE TO THE IRS

The housing allowance or fair rental value of a parsonage is not reported for income tax purposes to the IRS either on a W-2 form for ministers who are employees or on a Form 1099 for pastors who are self-employed, because it is not compensation subject to income tax. Of course, a record of expenditures must be kept. On the minister's tax return, only any unused allowance is reported as "other income."

For purposes of computing social security self-employment tax, any housing or furnishings allowance and the fair rental value of the parsonage, plus utilities paid by the congregation, are included in taxable income.

7

Social Security for Ministers

Social security is *social* insurance. It is a plan whereby the wealthy help pay for the benefits of the poor, those who live only a short time pay for the benefits of those who live a long time, and current workers provide the funds to pay the benefits for retirees. It is not *insurance* in the usual sense of the term. An individual's benefit is not necessarily related to the *premiums* paid. Most people, however, will collect their social security benefits because, as a result of increasing life expectancy rates, most people do live for many years beyond the normal retirement age.

CONSCIENTIOUS EXEMPTION FROM SOCIAL SECURITY

I am alarmed at the number of ministers who have voluntarily elected not to be covered by the social security program. Yes, the cost is high—15.3 percent beginning in 1990. For a minister with $30,000 of taxable income, that's an annual tax of $4,590, a lot of money for a benefit that could conceivably never be realized. On the other hand, the program may return much more than its costs. It all depends on how long one lives.

In 1937, the first workers eligible for participation in social security entered into the plan (the maximum annual employee tax was $30!). Beginning in 1951, churches and other nonprofit organizations could waive their exemption and begin withholding and paying taxes on wages paid to nonordained employees. Then, in 1955, ministers could for the first time waive their exemption (irrevocably) and begin participation in the program. In 1968, all ministers were *required* to pay the social security tax unless they opted out on grounds of religious principles or conscientious objection to governmental insurance and did so within two years (or, for those ordained after 1968, within two years of ordination and having ministerial earnings). Ministers who had previously elected to participate (after 1954) were required to continue.

This chapter is adapted from "Social Security for Clergy," by Manfred Holck Jr. and Robert J. Myers, *Lutheran Partners*, May/June 1986. Copyright 1986 by Augsburg Publishing House, Minneapolis. Used by permission of the authors.

Form 4361 exemption.

Reasons for opting out.

Ministers pay the social security self-employment tax rather than the employee social security tax, even though the IRS generally considers clergy to be employees for income tax purposes.

To request an exemption from social security, a minister must file with the IRS its Form 4361, "Application for Exemption from Self-Employment Tax for Use by Ministers, Members of Religious Orders and Christian Science Practitioners." An exemption is granted only on the basis of religious principles or conscientious objection to participation in governmental insurance programs such as social security. The forms must be filed by April 15 following the second year in which at least $400 of net income has been received from the ministry. If granted, the revocation cannot be changed, and the minister is then forever excluded from all social security benefits, based on his or her earnings in the ministry, including the hospital insurance portion of Medicare. However, these clergy may obtain the hospital insurance benefits (1) based on nonministerial earnings, for a required number of quarters, (2) from the spouse's earnings, or (3) by purchasing them from the government at a high premium ($234 per month per person in 1988).

Under present law, there is no opportunity or "window" time for revoking that exemption-request decision. (Such a temporary "window" was opened by legislation in 1977 for two years and again in 1986 until April 15, 1988.) Under current law, when you're out of social security, you are out for good.

It is hard to see how very many ministers could conscientiously oppose social security, especially because few denominations have ever expressed concern over social security legislation. Of course, any pastor could be opposed for individual reasons of conscience even though his or her denomination has no doctrine forbidding such belief. Since the Form 4361 must be signed in order to request exemption, ministers can perjure themselves if they claim conscientious objection, yet have no ethical basis for supporting that conviction.

Considerations of financial dissatisfaction or political philosophy, therefore, are not appropriate reasons for filing Form 4361. Contention that the tax contribution is too much and that similar benefits may be available from a private insurance company, or that social security is going broke, or that the tax for ministers is unfair, or that salary is just too low to afford the payment are not conscientious objections. The reason must be based on conscience or religious principle. Conscientious objection would include, for example, a belief that the members of the group—the church—should take care of their own and that government handouts from taxes paid by others should not be accepted by a member of that group to meet their needs. (Note that ministers who have been in military service at some time and are continuing GI insurance cannot honestly say that they are opposed to government insurance.)

The results of a recent survey among clergy members of a church pension plan (with 79 percent of those queried responding) revealed that 9.6 percent of the respondents were *not* participating in the social security program. Of the nearly 10 percent not in social security, 30 percent were under age 35. Only 40 percent said that they had arranged for alternate disability benefit insurance. Only 43 percent were concerned enough about their families to have made other financial arrangements for their survivors at their death. Although 63 percent had done something about replacing potential social security retirement benefits, only 14 percent had made any arrangements to fund the purchase of health insurance in lieu of Medicare after age 65. (It is difficult, however, to see how such funding would be possible, even for those few who believed that they could plan for postretirement health costs. It is virtually impossible to know now what future health-care costs and premiums are going to be.)

It is apparent that many clergy, especially younger ones, have not been aware of the basis for a valid waiver of participation and the serious financial consequences that an exemption from social security may create for them and their families. Because it is unlikely that comparable coverage can be secured and continuously maintained to replace the benefits available from social security, clergy who opt out are simply creating for themselves and their families potential personal financial difficulties.

If You Are Out

Ministers who secure an exemption from social security face significant economic challenges in replacing lost benefits.

1. Health insurance benefits provided by a denomination health-care plan in retirement when Medicare is not available are possible but can be very expensive. (In one denominational health plan in which benefits after age 65 are coordinated with Medicare, rates were $6,426 annually for husband and wife over age 65 who are not eligible for Medicare.) **Higher costs.**

2. Not only will contributions to an annuity plan have to be sufficient to replace an ever-increasing social security retirement benefit, but a personal plan would also need to provide an annual cost-of-living increase once benefits commence—virtually an impossible benefit. An insurance company will not guarantee, for many years, an interest rate anywhere near equal to current investment earnings nor provide a cost-of-living increase (without an expensive additional premium). **COLA increases.**

3. Premiums for a disability plan will need to be sufficient to guarantee a substantial benefit payment (including an annual cost-of-living increase) up to age 65.

4. Sufficient life insurance coverage will need to be purchased in order to provide pension incomes to a surviving spouse and young children.

Social security is our country's basic floor-of-insurance protection plan. Most denominations have built their pension plans on the **Basic insurance plan.**

premise that a minister is participating in social security. Retirement, disability, survivor, and health insurance benefits, which are almost impossible to duplicate with private insurance, are provided by social security. With so many benefits now potentially available, it seems foolish to forego the program.

ADVANTAGES OF SOCIAL SECURITY

Where will you get an annual automatic cost-of-living increase on your retirement benefit income? Certainly not from a denominational board of pensions or a commercial insurance company—only from social security.

Where can you find the disability and survivor pensions available in social security at the same cost?

And where will you get guaranteed affordable retirement health insurance? The church may guarantee lifetime health coverage for its ministers, but benefits under that coverage are coordinated with Medicare. Without Medicare, the church's plan would require a substantial increase in premium cost. Medicare Part A hospital coverage costs the eligible person nothing after age 65, aside from applicable deductibles.

Medicare.

The combination of Medicare and a denomination's health insurance plan generally means very small out-of-pocket health-care costs. As mentioned before, Medicare Part A costs participants in social security nothing. Part B of Medicare is available to anyone, even if he or she is not under social security, and is primarily for physician care. It requires a premium, currently (in 1990) $28.60 monthly (with about 75 percent of the cost being paid from the government's general revenue funds).

Depending on salary levels during a working career, ministers who are out of the system will also miss out on social security retirement benefits, which are often equal to 30 to 50 percent of their last year's salary (assuming a continuous salary history).

Social security is not a perfect plan, but it is one of the best worldwide. It will continue to be in existence as long as those responsible for its maintenance want to be reelected to Congress. If there are future problems, the plan will be rescued, as it has been previously. The social security taxes that you and I pay are placed in the Social Security Trust Fund, from which all benefits are paid. Congress has been advised by social security actuaries that the current tax rates will be satisfactory to meet expected benefit payments into the mid-21st century, unless Congress arbitrarily liberalizes benefits or the rate of inflation escalates more rapidly than wages rise.

SOCIAL SECURITY COSTS

The program's tax rate will continue to go up. In the Social Security Amendments of 1983, Congress provided that the self-employment

(SECA) social security tax must be double that of an employee. For too long, said Congress, self-employed persons paid too little into the trust fund. Through 1989 a tax credit has been applicable, so the actual self-employment rate has been less than double the combined employer-employee rate. Beginning in 1990, the self-employment tax will be at its projected maximum under current law. That tax, however, will be partially offset by a business-expense deduction for half the tax.

New social security calculation rules.

In the 1983 amendments, the tax rate had to be increased because the level of benefits had risen so greatly in 1979 through 1982. During that time, prices rose much more rapidly than wages, whereas the reverse had been expected (the same situation is occurring at present).

For 1990, the maximum earnings base on which social security taxes had to be paid was $51,300. The base will rise automatically in the future as the general level of wages rises throughout the nation.

BENEFIT CALCULATION

Social security benefits are calculated as follows: All earnings upon which the social security tax has been paid since 1951 (either as an employee or self-employed) are listed (up to the annual maximum taxable amount only). These earnings are then *indexed* by multiplying each year's taxable earnings by the ratio of (1) the nationwide average wage for the second year preceding the year of attainment of age 62* to (2) such average wage for the particular year. The earnings for the number of years that are the highest, equal to the years beginning with 1956 (or the year of attaining age 27, if later) through the year before attaining 62,* are totaled and averaged on a monthly basis. All years with earnings from 1951 on (including years *after* attaining age 62) are considered. The result is called the Average Indexed Monthly Earnings (AIME). By using a table of social security primary insurance amounts (PIA), one can determine the amount of social security benefit available for retirement at age 62 or later.*

AIME.

PIA.

Generally, the greater one's earnings, the lower the benefits received from social security as a *percentage* of earnings. Consider a worker who had always earned the maximum amount of wages subject to the social security tax. If retirement is at age 65 (the normal retirement age until 2003, then gradually increasing to age 67 in 2027), benefits for the individual would be about 27 percent of those earnings. Of course, if earnings are in excess of the maximum, the percentage relating benefits to total earnings would be less. If a person had a steady income of about 50 percent of the maximum earnings base, the social security benefit replacement ratio would be about 39 percent of the final level of pay. If earnings were equal to

Average benefit replacement ratio is 42%.

---
*Or disablement or death, if before age 62.

the average U.S. wage, benefits would be equal to about 42 percent of the last year's pay.

Benefits.

The maximum benefit (which was $975 a month for a worker attaining age 65 in 1990) applies for a worker who has paid tax on the maximum earnings base each year and who retires at age 65. Of course, a worker can receive a larger benefit by working beyond age 65. For retirement at age 62, a 20 percent reduction is currently applicable.

In addition to the worker's benefit, the spouse may receive a benefit of half of the worker's benefit at age 65 if the worker is retired and both husband and wife are age 65. A percentage reduction would be applicable for a spouse applying for benefits before reaching age 65. At age 62, the earliest age at which a spouse can receive benefits, the reduction is 25 percent—that is, 25 percent of half of the worker's age 65 benefit. A widow or widower, on the other hand, can receive benefits as early as age 60, but the benefit reduction is then 28½ percent.

If the spouse has also been employed and will receive a greater benefit as a worker than that coming from the other spouse, the larger benefit is paid. At the death of either spouse, the survivor receives the greater of the benefit based on his or her own earnings record or the widow/widower benefit; its amount, when first claimed at normal retirement age, is usually the benefit that the retired worker was receiving for herself or himself.

Working during retirement.

Persons who continue working to some extent after retirement may earn as much as $6,840 in 1990 when under age 65 without any reduction in benefits. During ages 65 to 69, up to $9,360 may be earned without any benefit reduction. There is no earnings limit at age 70 and over. Payments from the church's pension plans do not affect social security benefits. Income taxes in retirement, of course, are affected by earnings, pension payments, or both.

It is interesting to note that a self-employed worker who has always paid the maximum social security tax will, if retired in 1990 at age 65, recover the entire social security tax cost paid for those benefits in about five and a half years (not counting either the cost of money—that is, interest for all those years on the tax—or annual cost-of-living increases after age 65). If a spouse, also age 65, receives benefits, recovery of costs occurs in three and a half years. Total self-employment taxes paid for 1951 through 1990 are $65,667. The maximum benefit for a worker retiring at age 65 in 1990 is $975 monthly; with a spouse the same age, it is $1,463 monthly. Thus, $65,667 divided by $975 equals 67.4 months (five and a half years), or divided by $1,463 equals 44.9 months (three and a half years). The table on page 67 shows the tax rate paid through 1990. The table on page 68 shows the estimated benefits to be expected.

SOCIAL SECURITY TAXES

(Including Old-Age, Survivors, and Disability Insurance [OASDI]
and Hospital Insurance [HI])

Years	Employer and Employee Tax Rate	Self-Employed Tax Rate	Maximum Amount of Earnings Taxed Annually	Employee Maximum Annual Tax	Self-Employed Maximum Annual Tax
1937–49	1.00%	*	$ 3,000	$ 30.00	*
1950	1.50	*	3,000	45.00	*
1951–53	1.50	2.25%	3,600	54.00	$ 81.00
1954	2.00	3.00	3,600	72.00	108.00
1955–56	2.00	3.00	4,200	84.00	126.00
1957–58	2.25	3.375	4,200	94.50	141.75
1959	2.50	3.75	4,800	120.00	180.00
1960–61	3.00	4.50	4,800	144.00	216.00
1962	3.125	4.70	4,800	150.00	225.60
1963–65	3.625	5.40	4,800	174.00	259.20
1966	4.20	6.15	6,600	277.20	405.90
1967	4.40	6.40	6,600	290.40	422.40
1968	4.40	6.40	7,800	343.20	499.20
1969–70	4.80	6.90	7,800	374.40	538.20
1971	5.20	7.50	7,800	405.60	585.00
1972	5.20	7.50	9,000	468.00	675.00
1973	5.85	8.00	10,800	631.80	864.00
1974	5.85	7.90	13,200	772.20	1,042.80
1975	5.85	7.90	14,100	824.85	1,113.90
1976	5.85	7.90	15,300	895.05	1,208.70
1977	5.85	7.90	16,500	965.25	1,303.50
1978	6.05	8.10	17,700	1,070.85	1,433.70
1979	6.13	8.10	22,900	1,403.77	1,854.90
1980	6.13	8.10	25,900	1,587.67	2,097.90
1981	6.65	9.30	29,700	1,975.05	2,762.10
1982	6.70	9.35	32,400	2,170.80	3,029.40
1983	6.70	9.35	35,700	2,391.90	3,337.95
1984	6.70**	11.30	37,800	2,532.60	4,271.40
1985	7.05	11.80	39,600	2,791.80	4,672.80
1986	7.15	12.30	42,000	3,003.00	5,166.00
1987	7.15	12.30	43,800	3,131.70	5,387.40
1988	7.51	13.02	45,000	3,379.50	5,859.00
1989	7.51	13.02	48,000	3,604.80	6,249.60
1990+	7.65	15.30***	51,300	3,924.45	7,848.90

Total for 20 years (1971–1990)				37,380	60,763
Total for 25 years (1966–1990)				39,487	63,021
Total for 39 years (1951–1990)				41,261	65,667
Total for 53 years (1937–1990)				41,696	65,669

* No self-employed were included until 1951; clergy and farmers in 1955; lawyers, dentists, etc., in 1957; physicians in 1965.

** Employers paid 7.00% in 1984.

*** An income tax deduction as business expense is allowed with respect to half of the self-employment social security tax.

ESTIMATED MONTHLY BENEFITS IN 1990

Age in 1990	Benefit Recipient	\$12,000	\$20,000	\$30,000	\$40,000	\$51,300+
				Your Present Annual Earnings		
Retirement at Age 65						
65	You	$491	$683	$886	$938	$975
65	Spouse	245	341	443	469	487
62	You	$497	$690	$898	$955	$1,000
62	Spouse	248	345	449	477	500
Disability						
64	You	$484	$673	$873	$922	$957
	Child or Child & Spouse	242	336	436	461	478
60	You	$494	$685	$888	$938	$972
	Child or Child & Spouse	247	342	444	469	486
Survivors						
65	Spouse, 65	$491	$683	$886	$938	$975
	Spouse, 60	351	488	634	670	697
	Child*	368	512	665	703	731
60	Spouse, 65	$494	$685	$888	$938	$972
	Spouse, 60	353	490	635	671	694
	Child*	370	514	666	703	729

*Also applicable to spouse age 61 or under caring for eligible child (under age 16 or disabled before 22).

Source: Dale R. Detlefs and Robert J. Myers, *1990 Guide to Social Security*. (Louisville, Ky.: William M. Mercer-Meidinger, Inc.)

Be certain that any wages upon which you have paid tax (secular or ministerial wages) have been properly credited to your social security earnings record. Send Social Security Administration Form 7004 (which may be obtained at your local social security office) to the Social Security Administration in Baltimore, MD 21203, every three years. Usually errors can be corrected only within the previous 39½ months since wages were reported. As you near age 62, you can also ask for an estimate of your benefits (telephone 1 (800) 937-7005).

There's no denying that the tax bite for social security is very large, and as salary grows, the tax will increase. It is becoming more and more difficult, therefore, for some ministers, especially those on low pay schedules, to meet the commitments for this tax. To help with this burgeoning insurance cost, request that your congregation give you an allowance for part of the social security taxes you have to pay. (Only the minister, not the church, can pay the self-employment tax.) Such an allowance will be fully taxable for both income tax and social security tax purposes. The allowance can be any amount, but it should at least be equal to the FICA employer tax that the congregation would have had to pay on the minister's wage if he or she were considered an employee for social security purposes—7.65 percent beginning in 1990. Out-of-pocket costs for social security, after taxes on the allowance, may then be approximately the same as other employees incur.

A social security allowance.

8

Planning Retirement Income

Often, many older persons fear that they will outlive their assets, especially if one spouse must be in a nursing home. That is a legitimate concern. Modern medical science has extended life expectancy for many of us to the extent that great care must be taken to be certain our assets last as long as we do.

Younger pastors may not give retirement matters a second thought; by their mid-fifties, older pastors are giving much thought to it. Yet the time to begin planning for retirement income is in one's mid-twenties, not mid-fifties. Knowing that income needs may extend for another twenty years or more past retirement makes early and effective planning for retirement income essential. By beginning your retirement planning early, (1) you avoid last-minute decisions or changes to which little thought was given, (2) you take advantage of compound interest for many years to increase your savings account, and (3) you ease the frustrations and uncertainties often associated with actual retirement.

Begin retirement income planning early.

There's more to retirement planning than just income, however. By the time you retire, you must have answers to at least three concerns: what you are going to do, where you are going to live, and how much income you'll have whenever you do retire.

Retirement is not—or should not be—a decision to suddenly just do nothing. You don't work hard one day and then quit everything the next. You must remain active and busy. Responsibilities may be fewer and job pressures gone, but you can't do nothing and expect to live for very long.

What will you do?

Thus ministers need to develop other interests, but planning what you will do must begin long before you retire. Now is the time to cultivate those interests—stamp collecting, fishing, camping, music, writing, volunteer service projects, a new trade or business. Search out what suits you best and then dive into it for awhile. Try out several activities until you may discover talents you never knew that you had.

Also, thought needs to be given to retirement housing needs—beginning now. But most of all, retirement income needs careful, immediate attention.

70

Planning Retirement Income 71

SOURCES OF RETIREMENT INCOME

You may enjoy as many as six different sources of retirement income. Do you have any idea of your potential income from each? At age 30 your probably don't, but by age 55 or 60, you surely should.

Church Pension Plan

Almost all clergy participate in a denominational pension plan. Certainly all of the larger church groups have plans; smaller groups may not. Church pension-plan benefits differ substantially. That's because all plans have differing rules, and some plans are so new that they cannot offer many benefits as yet. A fully mature pension plan is one that's been around for at least forty years, thus giving even the oldest clergy in the group a chance to participate throughout a lifetime professional career.

Church pension plans are either defined-contribution or defined-benefit plans. In a defined-contribution plan, the amount of contribution required from the pastor and the congregation is stated. The resulting total accumulation is then used to purchase a lifetime annuity/pension. In a defined-benefit plan, all ministers are promised a pension of so many dollars depending on their number of years in the ministry, their age, or their salary. Such plans often require extensive fund-raising appeals within the churches to secure the money to pay the promised benefits.

In a defined-contribution plan, every participant's contribution is carefully retained by the plan, and the plan will pay an annuity at some future date. In this way, every member's pension is always fully funded and the promised payout of benefits is always possible. Defined-benefit plans, in contrast, can often be underfunded, and participants may not receive the full benefits promised. Funds accumulate only as congregations make voluntary contributions.

To fund your pension, your pension board may require the contribution of a percentage of salary or a flat dollar amount each month. Some funds require up to an 18 percent salary contribution. Naturally, the greater the contribution, the better for your retirement income, at least with a defined-contribution plan. When your pension is based on years of service, however, more contributions from you aren't very helpful financially.

The larger the pension contribution the better.

It is important that you review your potential benefits with your pension board periodically. Keeping current with the status of your plan will reassure you that all is well, at least with that portion of your retirement income.

Tax-Sheltered and Tax-Deferred Annuities

A tax-sheltered annuity (TSA) or tax-deferred annuity (TDA) plan will provide you with additional retirement income. Because most pension plans are TSA or TDA plans anyway, you can probably just

TSAs.

add to your accumulations with an additional salary-reduction contribution, although perhaps a separate TSA or TDA will be desirable or required. Only employees of nonprofit organizations can participate in a TSA or TDA plan. That's why ministers who claim to be employees are eligible for a TDA plan, but self-employed ministers are not.

In a TSA or TDA plan, your congregation either pays the contribution for you as a benefit or reduces salary to fund the payment. The money may be put into your pension plan or some insurance company plan. Whatever the approved recipient, your congregation makes the payments on your behalf; you cannot contribute directly to a TSA or TDA personally. Those contributions made on your behalf are then tax deferred; in other words, you pay no income tax or social security tax on the contribution from your congregation until after you retire. Furthermore, the interest income that those TSA or TDA plans earn is also not yet subject to income tax.

When you retire and stop making payments into the plan, you will begin to receive payments or an annuity. An annuity is a periodic, regular payment made to you for a designated length of time or for the rest of your life. Whenever you retire, the annuity that becomes part of your retirement income is generally fully taxable for income tax purposes (although it may be designated as housing allowance by the pension board and thus be potentially excludable). It is not subject to social security tax, however.

Social Security

Social security benefits can be substantial.

Review Chapter 7.

As noted in Chapter 7, social security benefits can be substantial. In 1990, a 65-year-old retired worker who has a 65-year-old spouse and who has always paid the maximum tax would have received a monthly pension of $1,463. A clergy couple earning only half the maximum would have had a monthly benefit of about $1,329. In subsequent years, benefits will increase because of wage indexing.

To maximize your social security benefits, it is important that you calculate your social security taxable income correctly. Income that is subject to the social security tax includes the following: base salary; housing (either the fair rental value of the parsonage plus utilities or any housing allowance received); car allowance reduced by car expenses; professional expenses allowance reduced by expenses; and any honoraria, fees, or royalties. Contributions to a TSA or TDA plan are generally not subject to the social security tax, but contributions to an IRA (to be discussed next) are subject to the tax. You know from Chapter 6 that housing is not subject to income tax under Section 107 of the Internal Revenue Code but is subject to self-employment social security tax.

Individual Retirement Account

An IRA offers further opportunity to increase retirement income and to reduce current taxable income at the same time. Present law (1989)

IRAs. permits a working individual (with adjusted gross income of less than $40,000 on a joint return) to deduct up to a $2,000-a-year contribution to an IRA. When both spouses earn at least $2,000 each, both may make the contribution. When only one spouse is employed, $2,250 is permitted.

The importance of the IRA is that the full amount can be invested before any deduction for tax is taken. The interest is tax deferred as well. Thus, the funds can compound at the maximum possible rate. Only when the account is withdrawn is any income tax due. (The IRA may be withdrawn after age 59½ without penalty, but required withdrawal must begin by age 70½.) Social security tax was paid on the contribution prior to its deduction on the tax return, so it is not due on withdrawal.

IRA funds can be invested in a variety of ways, and the owner maintains control. Certificates of deposit (CDs) at local banks, money market mutual funds or other mutual funds, real estate trusts, and insurance annuities are all possible investment vehicles.

If you are a minister not yet participating in an IRA, you should seriously consider getting involved promptly. It's an excellent way to build up retirement income. Even on a small salary, the discipline of saving something regularly will pay off handsomely by allowing a more carefree retirement. The 1986 Tax Reform Act did limit potential contributions to an IRA by high-earning taxpayers. On a joint return with adjusted gross income less than $40,000, $2,000 for each person is acceptable and deductible. For those participating in an employer-sponsored pension plan with an adjusted gross income over $50,000, no contribution is deductible, although interest is tax deferred. Between $40,000 and $50,000 the deduction is phased out.

Keogh Plans

Keogh retirement plans are much the same as IRAs, but they are reserved for the self-employed. Thus, salary from ministry is not eligible for Keogh plan consideration, says the IRS. Up to 20 percent of self-employment income—fees, honoraria, and royalties—can be placed in a Keogh plan. Restrictions on withdrawal and payout requirements are similar to IRAs.

Investments

Individual investments offer an important source of added retirement income for clergy able and disciplined enough to stick with carefully defined goals. Please review Chapter 4 for information about suggested investment strategies for ministers.

Other Sources of Income

Most ministers receive a salary increase each year. Putting that increase into savings for retirement and living on the previous year's salary amount can generate more retirement income. Obtaining a second job, writing, or somehow securing another source of income boosts net asset growth and potential retirement income even more when the extra money is invested and not spent. It is true that what we spend generally rises to the level of our income unless we deliberately put those extra dollars aside.

Insurance

Some clergy are "insurance poor," but most clergy probably have too little insurance when they are young and too much when they are older. (Look again at Chapter 5 on insurance.)

Do you need life insurance after retirement?

Generally, you should secure as much insurance as possible when your children are young. Term insurance will offer the most coverage for the least cost at that time. The older you become and the less pressing your financial responsibilities to dependents are, the less life insurance you need. Thus, as you approach retirement, it is often wise to reduce your cost and improve your investments. That generally means that as soon as your children are grown, you can do one of several things with your permanent policies. You can borrow the maximum amount possible at a low interest rate and invest it at a higher rate. You can cash in the policy and invest the proceeds. You can stop paying premiums and take paid-up insurance. Or, if you're ready to retire, you can purchase an annuity with your insurance policy's cash value, thus securing a regular income for the rest of your life.

As for dividends from mutual life insurance companies, these are not taxable income until the dividends exceed premiums. You may leave them with the company to earn a low rate of interest, you may take them in cash and invest them yourself at a higher rate, you may purchase additional paid-up insurance, or you may use the dividends to pay your premiums.

PLANNING RETIREMENT HOUSING

Right now you have housing, whether you live in a parsonage or own or rent your home. At retirement, however, your current arrangements may change drastically. At that time you might be out looking for your own home, especially if you've been in a parsonage all your life. Of course, homeowning clergy can stay put, but because your housing needs change as you grow older, that might not be best. Selling your current home and moving to a smaller house or apartment may be required. Now is the time to begin planning for that event.

You may wish to move to a new location, possibly because you want less winter or you wish to be closer to family and friends. Carefully review your reasons for wanting to move and be certain that it is the best step to take. Renting on a temporary basis gives you an opportunity to change your mind easily should things not work out as you had hoped.

With homeownership in retirement, the same rules apply with respect to a housing allowance as during active ministry. Your pension can be designated as housing allowance and you can exclude it from taxable income to the extent that you use it to provide for a home in retirement. Whether you rent or buy makes no difference.

Tax Matters Concerning Housing

All ordained ministers who are either active parish pastors, employed by an agency or institution under the control of the church, or retired enjoy the benefits of Section 107 of the Internal Revenue Code as fully explained in Chapter 6. That benefit excludes from taxable income the value of church-owned housing or a housing allowance to the extent that it is used to provide a home. Because it is such a substantial tax savings, maximizing use of the housing allowance exclusion is very important for saving tax dollars now as well as during retirement.

Revenue Ruling 75-22 allows a church denominational pension board to designate pensions as housing allowance. Retired clergy enjoy the same tax benefits as parish pastors with respect to the use of a housing allowance. The minister's denominational pension board will probably designate all of the pension as a housing allowance; thus, to the extent that the pension issued is used to provide a home, it is excludable from income tax. This means that retired home-owning clergy may want to retain their home mortgages as long as possible to achieve the largest possible exclusion. Retired ministers who have their homes paid for won't be able to exclude as much of their pension because their housing costs are lower. They will pay more income tax than retired clergy who have large mortgages on their homes.

TAXES BEFORE AND AFTER RETIREMENT

Most taxpayers are eager to pay as little tax as possible. Ministers are no exception. Income taxes prior to retirement will usually be substantially more than after retirement. Searching out all the possible ways to reduce taxes on income now and defer them until retirement will save you money.

Taxable income in retirement will probably be much less than it is during active ministry. Social security taxes are no longer due except on any continued part-time earnings, and social security benefits are generally not taxable.* The pension housing allowance is not

---

*For wealthier retirees, income tax could be due on up to one-half of social security benefits. If the sum of adjusted gross income, tax-exempt interest, and one-half of social security benefits exceeds $32,000 on a joint return, income tax is due on the lesser of one-half of social security taxes or the difference between $32,000 and total income so computed.

taxable when used to provide a home. Payments to TSAs, IRAs, and your pension fund stop. Thus, even though income from IRAs, TSAs, and perhaps an equity fund and other investment is taxable, it is offset by the tax-free income and lower expenses.

Keep in mind that before retirement you pay the self-employment social security tax on your total income, including housing, that you are an employee for income tax purposes, and that your professional expenses are deducted only on Schedule A, with car expenses shown on Form 2106. When you retire your income may not be much less, but because more will be exempt from taxes, you'll have more take-home pay.

ESTATE PLANNING

Even with all the financial planning in the world, you might not make it to retirement. Yet, for your surviving spouse, that planning is very important. Make certain that your surviving spouse has a retirement income, too. Planning is also important if you're the surviving spouse. The best policy, if you're married, is to do your planning together. If you're single, let a trusted friend or relative in on your plans.

Let somebody know your plans.

Develop a notebook of instructions. List where everything is—wills, bankbooks, insurance policies, securities, tax returns for previous years, and so on (use Worksheet 7). List all that you own and owe—insurance policies, all securities, bank accounts, and retirement plans. Specify amounts, beneficiaries, addresses, contact persons, exceptions, and limitations. Explain settlement options and suggest choices. Write out instructions for funerals and list names and addresses of your accountant, attorney, banker, insurance representative, and broker (use Worksheet 8).

Then share the record keeping with your spouse. Both of you need to be familiar with procedures. Both of you should do a tax return, keep the checkbook, talk to the insurance representative and investment advisor, and go to the safe deposit box. After all, it's likely that someday one or the other of you will have to do it all alone. There's no better time to learn how than when you're both able to do so together.

A FINAL COMMENT

This has been a brief overview of the financial matters you'll need to consider as you approach retirement. This summary is intended to stimulate your thinking and arouse your interest in possibilities. It's also an attempt to warn you that a productive retirement requires setting goals, assessing needs, and *saving*. No matter what your age, it's never too soon to begin planning for retirement. You can anticipate a financially worry-free retirement when you plan, budget, invest, and take decisive action now.

Even though your finances may currently be on what seems to be shaky ground, with careful planning you will have them in good shape by retirement (and probably much sooner). I hope that all of these suggestions will be helpful and stimulating to your financial planning and that you will discover creative and useful ways to enjoy the incomes you receive.

CONCLUSION

This book has been addressed to ministers, and because ministers have not been traditionally well paid, I have to assume that some of you are having financial problems. I have tried to suggest things that you can do about these problems. Obviously, when the paycheck doesn't stretch, you must boost income or reduce spending (or both). You will need some one-on-one financial counseling to help you understand why you have the problems you do. Of course you spend too much, but why? Of course your income is too low, but why? Of course you spend as much as you earn, but why?

If you've gone through these pages and can't find anything that will be helpful, if you are unwilling to change what you do, or can't get started on your own, please get some professional advice. (Note the discussion in Chapter 2 on selecting a financial advisor.)

I am convinced that any ministerial family can solve its financial problems with sufficient determination and resolve (and sometimes a little help from others). Many have, and many more will. Your family can, too.

All best wishes in your search for financial freedom. Use your common sense about what you spend and be realistic and honest when making your budget, but don't forget to set goals and work to achieve them. You can make it.

Bibliography

Chakour, Charles. *Building the Clergyman's Compensation.* Nashville: Abingdon Press, 1987.

Hammer, Richard R. *Pastor, Church and Law.* Springfield, Mo.: Gospel Publishing House, 1983.

Holck, Manfred. *Tax Planning for Clergy.* Englewood Cliffs, N.J.: Prentice-Hall, 1989.

Markstein, David L. *Manage Your Money and Life Better.* New York: McGraw-Hill, 1971.

Morgan, Darold H. *Personal Finances for Ministers.* Nashville: Broadman Press, 1985.

Northcutt, David L. *Financial Management for Clergy.* Grand Rapids, Mich.: Baker Book House, 1984.

Porter, W. Thomas. *Touche Ross Guide to Personal Financial Management.* Englewood Cliffs, N.J.: Prentice-Hall, 1989.

Soled, Alex J. *The Essential Guide to Wills, Estates, Trusts, and Death Taxes.* Glenview, Ill.: Scott, Foresman and Co. and American Association of Retired Persons, 1984.

Weaver, Peter, and Annette Buchanan. *What to Do with What You've Got.* Glenview, Ill.: Scott, Foresman and Co. and American Association of Retired Persons, 1984.

Table 1
Investment Evaluation Checklist*

	Div	Liq	Saf	CI	FA	TA	Lev	Mgmt
Savings A/C	Poor	Good	Good	Good	Poor	Poor	Poor	Good
CD	Poor	Good	Good	Good	Poor	Poor	Poor	Good
T-bill	Poor	Fair	Good	Good	Poor	Fair	Poor	Good
Treasury note**	Poor	Fair	Good	Good	Poor	Fair	Poor	Good
Savings bonds***	Poor	Good	Good	Poor	Poor	Fair	Poor	Good
Agency securities	Poor	Fair	Good	Good	Poor	Poor	Poor	Good
Money market–mutual fund	Poor	Good	Fair	Good	Poor	Poor	Poor	Good
Mutual fund–growth stock	Fair	Good	Poor	Poor	Good	Fair	Fair	Fair
Mutual fund–income fund	Fair	Good	Poor	Fair	Fair	Poor	Fair	Fair
Mutual fund–bond fund	Fair	Good	Poor	Fair	Fair	Poor	Fair	Fair
Municipal bonds	Fair	Poor	Fair	Good	Poor	Good	Fair	Poor
Common stocks	Good	Poor	Poor	Poor	Good	Fair	Fair	Poor
Corporate bonds	Good	Poor	Fair	Fair	Poor	Poor	Fair	Poor
Real estate	Fair	Poor	Fair	Poor	Good	Fair	Good	Poor
Collectibles	Fair	Poor	Poor	Poor	Fair	Poor	Poor	Poor

Div = Diversification — Can the investment be diversified among a variety of securities?

Liq = Liquidity

Saf = Safety

CI = Current income — This is the evaluation of the availability of current income, not the rate of return.

FA = Future appreciation

RA = Tax advantage — Is there potential for a tax-free income tax benefit?

Lev = Leverage — Is this security a good one to purchase on margin and earn more than the cost of borrowing?

Mgmt = Ease of management

*Reprinted from *Financial Management: A Workbook for Pastors* by Manfred Holck Jr. Copyright 1990 by Aid Association for Lutherans, Appleton, Wisconsin. Used by permission.
**Interest income from Treasury bills and Treasury notes is not subject to state income taxes.
***Savings bond income is only available at redemption. Interest income on EE series savings bonds is tax deferred to redemption or, if transferred to HH series, upon redemption of those new bonds.

Worksheet 1
Current Annual Income and Expenses

INCOME
Salary from congregation $_____
Housing allowance, if any _____
Other allowances _____
Honoraria, fees, and other income _____
Spouse's income _____
    Total income $_____

EXPENSES
Contributions $_____
Housing—mortage or rent _____
Household expenses (repairs, new furnishings) _____
Social security tax _____
Income tax _____
Food, snacks, and restaurants _____
Utilities—heat, electricity, phone, etc. _____
Transportation, including car payments _____
Insurance premiums _____
Medical bills, prescription drugs _____
Clothing, shoes, cleaning _____
Savings and investments _____
Recreation, fun, and entertainment _____
Personal allowances for family members _____
Gifts (Christmas, birthdays, etc.) _____
Education—parents and children _____
Miscellaneous (everything else; you may wish to list these by topic) _____
    Total expenses $_____

DIFFERENCE—PLUS OR MINUS $_____

Worksheet 2
Determining Your Net Worth

You need to know what you have and what you owe before you can determine insurance needs and retirement income possibilities, plan your estate, or borrow money at the bank.

LIST YOUR ASSETS
(This is what you have)

	Example	Your List
Checking account	$ 500	$
Savings accounts and C.D.s	5,000	
IRAs; annuities	2,250	
U.S. savings bonds	100	
Cash value of life insurance	1,000	
Pension plan accumulations	-0-	
Market value of residence	-0-	
Second home, other real estate	-0-	
Household furnishings	5,000	
Automobiles	2,000	
Jewelry, antiques, valuables	500	
Loans others owe you	-0-	
Other items you own	-0-	
Total assets	$ 16,350	$

LIST YOUR DEBTS
(This is what you owe to others)

Current charge accounts	$ 300	$
Installment debts	500	
Mortage loan	-0-	
(Monthly payment $ _____)		
Social security and income tax due	-0-	
Other loans (school, etc.)	15,000	
Total debts	$ 15,800	$

NET WORTH:
TOTAL ASSETS MINUS DEBTS $ 550 $

The Minister's Handbook for Personal Finance copyright © 1990 Augsburg Fortress.
This worksheet may be reproduced for personal use.

Worksheet 3

An Earnings-Savings-Spending Plan: The Budget

Month ____ Year ____   **Estimated**   **Actual**

INCOME
Salary from congregation $_____ $_____
Housing allowance, if any   _____   _____
Other allowances   _____   _____
Honoraria, fees, other income   _____   _____
Spouse's income   _____   _____
    Total income $_____ $_____

EXPENSES
Contributions $_____ $_____
Housing—mortgage or rent   _____   _____
Household expenses (repairs, new furnishings)   _____   _____
Social security tax   _____   _____
Income tax   _____   _____
Food, snacks, restaurants   _____   _____
Utilities—heat, electricity, phone   _____   _____
Transportation, including car payments   _____   _____
Insurance premiums   _____   _____
Medical bills, prescriptions   _____   _____
Clothing, shoes, cleaning   _____   _____
Savings and investments   _____   _____
Recreation, fun, entertainment   _____   _____
Personal allowances   _____   _____
Gifts (Christmas, birthdays, etc.)   _____   _____
Education—parents and children   _____   _____
Miscellaneous (everything else; you may wish to list   _____   _____
    these by topic)
    Total expenses $_____ $_____

BALANCE $_____ $_____

The Minister's Handbook for Personal Finance copyright © 1990 Augsburg Fortress.
This worksheet may be reproduced for personal use.

Worksheet 4
Current Debt Load

	Monthly Payments	Number of months to pay	Total due
Government education loans:			
College	$_____	_____	$_____
	_____	_____	_____
Seminary	_____	_____	_____
	_____	_____	_____
Church education loans:			
College	_____	_____	_____
	_____	_____	_____
Seminary	_____	_____	_____
	_____	_____	_____
Credit cards:			
Master Card	_____	_____	_____
Visa	_____	_____	_____
Other	_____	_____	_____
	_____	_____	_____
	_____	_____	_____
Personal loans from:			
Family	_____	_____	_____
Friends	_____	_____	_____
	_____	_____	_____
	_____	_____	_____
Installment loans	_____	_____	_____
	_____	_____	_____
	_____	_____	_____
Car loans	_____	_____	_____
	_____	_____	_____
	_____	_____	_____
Life insurance loans	_____	_____	_____

TOTAL DUE $_____

Total monthly payments $_____

Total annual payments
(12 times monthly payments) $_____

The Minister's Handbook for Personal Finance copyright © 1990 Augsburg Fortress.
This worksheet may be reproduced for personal use.

Worksheet 5

How Much Life Insurance Do You Need?

	Example	Your Estimate
Step One—What you already have		
1. List your net worth	$ 50,000	$
2. Deduct cash value of life insurance, pension accumulations, nonincome-producing assets (car, furniture)	−23,000	
3. Add face value of life insurance	25,000	
4. This is what your survivors would be able to invest to earn additional income if you died today	$ 52,000	$
Step Two—What you need		
5. Cash for estimated burial costs	$ 3,000	
6. Temporary emergency cash for family	2,000	
7. Education fund for your children	12,000	
8. Total immediate cash needs	$ 17,000	$
9. Annual income you want for spouse	$ 20,000	$
10. Minus social security benefits	−8,000	
11. Minus church pension-plan benefits	−7,000	
12. Net annual amount of additional income your survivors will need	$ 5,000	$
Step Three—Additional life insurance needed		
13. Divide line 12 by 0.10. This is how much principal you will need to invest at 10% to provide extra income over social security and pensions benefits	$ 50,000	$
14. Add your immediate cash needs	17,000	
15. Deduct what you already have	−52,000	
16. This is the additional insurance you will need for your survivors in order to provide for them the immediate cash, annual income, and lifetime annuity you want	$ 15,000	$

The Minister's Handbook for Personal Finance copyright © 1990 Augsburg Fortress.
This worksheet may be reproduced for personal use.

Worksheet 6
Record of Insurance Policies

	Home	Car	Life	Other
Policy Number	_____	_____	_____	_____
Insured	_____	_____	_____	_____
Beneficiary	_____	_____	_____	_____
Company	_____	_____	_____	_____
Type	_____	_____	_____	_____
Premium due date	_____	_____	_____	_____
Annual premium	_____	_____	_____	_____
Policy amount	_____	_____	_____	_____
Where is policy?	_____	_____	_____	_____
Status (current?)	_____	_____	_____	_____

The Minister's Handbook for Personal Finance copyright © 1990 Augsburg Fortress.
This worksheet may be reproduced for personal use.

Worksheet 7
Where Are Your Records?

Location

Husband's will _____

Wife's will _____

Trust agreements _____

Property deeds _____
_____

Mortgage documents _____
_____

Car titles _____ _____
_____

Stock certificates _____
_____

Bonds _____
_____

Certificates of deposit _____
_____

Checking accounts _____
_____

Savings accounts/passbooks _____
_____

Life insurance policies _____
_____
_____

Other insurance policies _____
_____

The Minister's Handbook for Personal Finance copyright © 1990 Augsburg Fortress.
This worksheet may be reproduced for personal use.

Retirement agreements _____

IRAs/Keogh plans _____

Church pension plan funds _____
_____

Birth certificates _____

Marriage license _____

Divorce papers _____

Notes due you _____

Notes due to others _____

Call/employment documents _____

Income tax returns _____ _____
_____ _____
_____ _____

Military documents _____

Net worth statements _____

Safe deposit box keys _____

Other records/valuables _____
_____ _____
_____ _____
_____ _____

Who has access to your safe deposit box? _____

Under whose name is your safe deposit box registered? _____

Worksheet 8
Names of Important People:

Attorney
Name: _____
Firm: _____

Address: _____
City, State: _____
Phone: _____

Name: _____
Firm: _____

Address: _____
City, State: _____
Phone: _____

Bank Officer
Name: _____
Firm: _____

Address: _____
City, State: _____
Phone: _____

Name: _____
Firm: _____

Address: _____
City, State: _____
Phone: _____

Investment Broker
Name: _____
Firm: _____

Address: _____
City, State: _____
Phone: _____

Name: _____
Firm: _____

Address: _____
City, State: _____
Phone: _____

Certified Public Accountant
Name: _____
Firm: _____

Address: _____
City, State: _____
Phone: _____

Name: _____
Firm: _____

Address: _____
City, State: _____
Phone: _____

Insurance Representative

Name: _____
Firm: _____

Address: _____
City, State: _____
Phone: _____

Name: _____
Firm: _____

Address: _____
City, State: _____
Phone: _____

Investment Advisor

Name: _____
Firm: _____

Address: _____
City, State: _____
Phone: _____

Name: _____
Firm: _____

Address: _____
City, State: _____
Phone: _____

Others

Name: _____
Firm: _____

Address: _____
City, State: _____
Phone: _____

Name: _____
Firm: _____

Address: _____
City, State: _____
Phone: _____

To which of these would you or someone responsible for your affairs turn to for an important financial decision? _____